A PERCUSSIONIST'S GUIDE TO MUSIC–BIBLIOGRAPHIC ESSAYS

Front cover illustration by George Gard.
Author Photo provided by the University of Wisconsin-Stevens Point,
News Services.

A PERCUSSIONIST'S GUIDE TO MUSIC– BIBLIOGRAPHIC ESSAYS

Geary Larrick

The Edwin Mellen Press
Lewiston•Queenston•Lampeter

Library of Congress Cataloging-in-Publication Data

Larrick, Geary, 1943-
   A percussionist's guide to music-bibliographic essays / Geary Larrick.
      p. cm.
   Includes bibliographical references and index.
   ISBN 0-7734-7301-7
      1. Percussion music--Bibliography. 2. Percussion instruments--Bibliography.

ML128.P23 L37 2002
786.8--dc21

                                                                    2001042789

A CIP catalog record for this book is available from the British Library.

The Edwin Mellen Press   The Edwin Mellen Press
Box 450   Box 67
Lewiston, New York   Queenston, Ontario
USA 14092-0450   CANADA L0S 1L0

The Edwin Mellen Press, Ltd.
Lampeter, Ceredigion, Wales
UNITED KINGDOM SA48 8LT

Printed in the United States of America

DEDICATION

To my daughter:
Sulina Larrick

Table of Contents

List of Illustrations

Preface

Scholarly books are sometimes written from the "ivory tower," an ideal location far removed from the actual world of their subject matter. Such is not the case with this book. Its author, Geary Larrick, is a hands-on percussionist, an advocate steeped in the practice and rituals of the percussion world. To an outsider, the word "percussionist" conjures up an immediate image of the most diverse, multifaceted musician of Western society, who performs on a diversity of instruments, both of specific and undetermined pitch, those of the classical tradition and those borrowed from popular and ethnic traditions. This is Geary Larrick. An insider, having completed degrees at The Ohio State University, Eastman School of Music, and the University of Colorado, he launched into a variegated career of teaching, and creative work, performing jazz, rock, fusion, Latin, marching band, of course, and the complete orchestral battery, with dozens of ensembles and orchestras in the academy and in the town, some of which he has directed or conducted. And he often performs as soloist. He has already been the venerable professor of percussion and author, yet also the improviser, band leader, arranger, and composer of an extensive repertoire which he has published with his own firm, G and L Publishing. When it comes to percussion, Geary Larrick has done it all, save constructing his own instruments. He is, then, a credible yet modest witness of the detail this volume covers.

This book is essentially a collection of valuable articles on the subject, an eclectic anthology of the observations of an expert in the field. It addresses Dr. Larrick's experiences and challenges, a summary of his other writings and percussion compositions, as well as the problems and the solutions he encountered during his career in the Upper Midwest. The solutions will be a guide to others, whether entering or in the midst of a career in percussion performance.

Dr. Larrick's new book surveys some of the percussion literature, and reviews performances--his own and those of other professionals. It is also a reference book. Its extensive bibliography of percussion-related topics and appropriate sources will be a starting point for investigating its many subjects through the percussion periodicals, methods, studies, and catalogues he reviews.

Percussion instruments sometimes become the protagonists of the story, including those representing ancient or ethnic societies: Mexico and Ecuador, India and China, Poland and Africa, Native America, jazz, instruments of the Bible, and so on. Those of special focus are cymbals, timpani, and components of the drum set. The reader will find coverage of two types of compositions: those of the classical tradition and those of percussionists. In the first category, for instance, there is mention of Ingolf Dahl, Norman Dello Joio, Paul Creston, Elliott Carter, John Cage, Darius Milhaud, and of course Bach and Beethoven. Some of the percussion composers are John Beck, Bob Becker, M. Ptaszynska, Clair Omar Musser, and Gary Burton. The reader will find many players, including women, far too many to itemize. This is a commendable book from an authority in the field.

Richard Pinnell (Ph.D., UCLA)
Chair, Department of Music
University of Wisconsin-La Crosse

Foreword

Although this book was written in 2000, production for publication is being done in 2001. Thus, it is a history of activity in percussion and music with sources primarily from the 20th Century.

Indeed, it is exciting to be a part of music history at the advent of the 21st Century. One might reflect about the beginnings of other new centuries, such as the years 1401 and 1901. This kind of practice requires solid grounding in the knowledge of history, and offers encouragement to the reader in regard to dealing with change.

The following several essays with three related artworks, present the reader with much information in bibliographic form with commentary. International and multicultural aspects of music are considered, as are a variety of points of view. The author hopes that the reader has as much fun perusing these pages, as the author did putting them together.

Acknowledgments

The encouragement for writing his book came from J. Rupnow. Collaborating artist is G. Gard. Of course, author's family, friends and colleagues were very instrumental in supporting activity leading to this volume. My 1968 Compilation was written at the request of Beck, published in the Journal of the National Association of College Wind and Percussion Instructors, reprinted in Percussive Notes. NACWPI and the Percussive Arts Society have given their permission to rewrite this material, and G. Gard has given me permission to include his art. The current address of PAS is 701 NW Ferris, Lawton, Oklahoma, where there is now a museum and library associated with percussion.

Several professionals contributed with assistance to the author in writing this book. These include, not exclusively, M. Van Chef, R. Weerts, N. Alburger, S. Maloney, L. Miller-Lachmann, E.J. Miller, R.P Wolensky, J.L. Moore, R. Pinnell, R Weiner, J. Baldwin, L. Pimentel, F.M. Combs, D. Elsenrath, M. Fang, S. Sundell, T. O'Malley, S Wanserski, D. Nixon, J. Adams, T. Peterson, S. Bergeron, T. O'Mahoney and W. England. The author is appreciative of these persons and their help in many projects. Photos of the author appear with the kind permission of the News Service Photography Division at the University of Wisconsin-Stevens Point.

Introduction

Writing this book is a celebration of anniversaries for the author. First, the year 2000 marks thirty years since graduating from the Eastman School of Music of the University of Rochester with the degree Master of Music in performance and literature.

Second, 2000 marks thirty-five years since graduating from The Ohio State University with a Bachelor of Science in music education. Memorable aspects of that experience include performing a recital in Hughes Hall Auditorium, and playing a featured marimba solo with the OSU Concert Band in the amphitheater near Mirror Lake.

Third, 2000 marks the fiftieth year that the author has played the keyboard percussion. This experience began at the age of seven with the purchase of a small studio size marimba from a department store in downtown Columbus, Ohio. A highlight of these experiences was playing before a stadium crowd on July 4 in the 1970s, while doing doctoral work at the University of Colorado in Boulder.

Indeed, these anniversaries are reason enough to research and review the author's knowledge about percussion music. A career full of rich experiences has included fifteen years singing baritone with the Chancel Choir at St. Paul's United Methodist Church in Stevens Point, Wisconsin, and twenty-five years as a performer with the Central Wisconsin Symphony Orchestra. Highlights of these presentations have included Easter presentations, and youth concerts with student soloists.

The publication of four previous books by this author in 1989, 1990, 1992 and 1999, builds certain skills that one can best gain from experience. Foremost among these is an interest and ability at the art and science of bibliography, especially with a creative approach.

Thus, the purpose of this book is to acquaint the reader with knowable facets of percussion music, derived from experience and study. Several of these aspects can transfer to other disciplines, and are not exclusive. Certainly the scholarly pursuit of knowledge within the field of percussion music has much in

1

common with similar areas in history, theory, pedagogy, education, art, philosophy and performance.

It is hoped that this volume of bibliographic essays can prove to be enlightening, enjoyable and melodious for the reader's intellect. The confluence of rhythm, melody, harmony, form and tone color in percussion music are likewise good for listening.

A Selected Bibliography

Beginning in 1968, the author has been writing for the National Association of College Wind and Percussion Instructors, with several articles appearing in the NACWPI Journal. Following are several of those publications referenced in standard bibliographic fashion, ranging from 1987 to 2000. The first article listed, on the marimba, was written at the University of Colorado in Boulder as a lecture recital, then presented at the University of Wisconsin-Stevens Point and at The Ohio State University in Columbus in May, 1986.

Larrick, Geary. "The Marimba as A Transcribing Instrument." NACWPI Journal XXXV/3 (Spring 1987), 13.

Larrick, Geary. "Elliott Carter and His Timpani Pieces." NACWPI Journal XXXVI/2 (Winter 1987-88), 22.

Larrick, Geary. "Percussion Music Reviews." NACWPI Journal XXXVI/3 (Spring 1988), 33.

Larrick, Geary. "On Musical Ability, Conducting and Analysis." NACWPI Journal XXXVII/3 (Spring 1989), 29.

Larrick, Geary. "Percussion Ensemble Reviews." NACWPI Journal XXXVII/4 (Summer 1989), 28.

Larrick, Geary. "Paul Creston and His Marimba Concerto." NACWPI Journal XXXVIII/1 (Fall 1989), 9.

Larrick, Geary. "Percussion Music Reviews." NACWPI Journal XXXVIII/3 (Spring 1990), 34.

Larrick, Geary. "Analysis of Percussion Music." NACWPI Journal XXXVIII/4 (Summer 1990), 13.

Larrick, Geary. "Multicultural Music: Bob Becker's 'Lahara'." NACWPI Journal XXXIX/1 (Fall 1990), 10.

Larrick, Geary. "Percussion Music Reviews." NACWPI Journal XXXIX/2 (Winter 1990-91), 26.

Larrick, Geary. "Guidelines for the Timpanist." NACWPI Journal XXXIX/3 (Spring 1991), 12.

3

Larrick, Geary. "Chamber Music Review." NACWPI Journal XXXIX/4 (Summer 1991), 30.

Larrick, Geary. "Music of Africa, Bali, China and the Xylophone." NACWPI Journal XL/2 (Winter 1991-92), 16.

Larrick, Geary. "Book Review." NACWPI Journal XL/2 (Winter 1991-92), 18.

Larrick, Geary. "Solo Timpani Review." NACWPI Journal XLI/2 (Winter 1992-93), 27.

Larrick, Geary. "Music as an Adjunct to Education." NACWPI Journal XLI/3 (Spring 1993), 11.

Larrick, Geary. "Compact Disc Reviews." NACWPI Journal XLI/4 (Summer 1993), 18.

Larrick, Geary. "Marimba Concerto Bibliography." NACWPI Journal XLII/1 (Fall 1993), 20.

Larrick, Geary. "Book Review." NACWPI Journal XLII/1 (Fall 1993), 38.

Larrick, Geary. "Bibliography on Ethics and Copyright." NACWPI Journal XLII/2 (Winter 1993-94), 20.

Larrick, Geary. "Percussion Music Reviews." NACWPI Journal XLII/3 (Spring 1994), 27.

Larrick, Geary. "Women Percussionists of the 20th Century." NACWPI Journal XLIII/3 (Spring 1995), 4.

Larrick, Geary. "Video Reviews." NACWPI Journal XLIII/4 (Summer 1995), 20.

Larrick, Geary. "Book Review." NACWPI Journal XLIII/4 (Summer 1995), 48.

Larrick, Geary. "Canadian and European Percussionists of the 20th Century." NACWPI Journal XLIV/1 (Fall 1995), 4.

Larrick, Geary. "Compact Disc Review." NACWPI Journal XLIV/3 (spring 1996), 28.

Larrick, Geary. "Compact Disc Review." NACWPI Journal XLIV/4 (Summer 1996), 42.

Larrick, Geary. "African-American Percussionists of the 20th Century." NACWPT Journal XLVI/1 (Fall 1997), 16.

Larrick, Geary. "Music for Keyboard Percussion." <u>NACWPI Journal</u> XLVII/1 (Fall 1998), 18.

Larrick, Geary. "Percussion in Music." <u>NACWPI Journal</u> XLVIII/1 (Fall 1999), 8.

Larrick, Geary. "Method Book Reviews." <u>NACWPI Journal</u> XLVIII/3 (Spring 2000), 31.

Study of the preceding bibliographic listing reveals a variety of subjects within percussion music. The number of percussion instruments worldwide is, of course, huge. Further, the number of types of percussion instruments is impressive. Thus, variety is the name of the game, so to speak.

The aspiring percussionist can learn the basics, such as good technique on the snare drum and marimba, then transfer to research and writing. Creative work, for example improvisation and music composition, is an additional area worth pursuing. Attaining success in a number of areas of percussion can be rewarding, stimulating, remunerative, helpful and pleasant.

A Short History of Percussion

It has been said that percussion instruments and percussion music are older than written history. This is probably true. Percussion is present in practically all cultures in the world, and the instruments are depicted on early art works.

The reader may be interested in a bibliographic survey of percussion music history. Indeed, the doctor of music degree with a major in percussion, present since about 1970, is a sign of growth in information in this field. Throughout this volume are printed many published citations in this regard.

It is the purpose of this essay to guide the reader through a maze of information, citing specific works that have to do with the history of percussion. First of all, one might wish to consult The Music Index, under the heading percussion. This can give the scholar an idea of what has been published, as well as sources and authors.

James Blades' percussion history book (Faber and Faber, 1984) is a giant in the field. Gordon Peters' Treatise on Percussion (published by Kemper-Peters) is detailed and enjoyable to read.

John Beck's Percussion Encyclopedia (New York, Garland), gives a comprehensive view from the end of the 20th Century, including many articles by specialists. In the year 2000, University of Wyoming percussion professor Stephen Barnhart has published with Greenwood Press a book on Percussionists, listing information about five hundred practitioners of the art.

This author has published books in 1989 (New York, Peter Lang), 1990, 1992 and 1999 (Lewiston, New York, Edwin Mellen) that deal primarily with percussion music and instruments. The 1990 book, entitled Musical References and Song Texts in the Bible, discusses other instruments including the voice, though that particular study began with a look at percussion citations in the Holy Bible. Thus, among the four volumes, percussion history is related from antiquity to the end of the 20th Century. Composers and performers are discussed, along with the music and instruments, in addition to teaching and performance.

Further, the dictionary of percussion by Adato and Judy has photos as well as text and an alphabetical listing of terms. The international Percussive Arts Society has published journals and newsletters since the 1960s, including much information and opinions of percussion writers. The French journal Percussions is highly recommended, as are the percussion articles in MGG and The New Grove. The NDA Magazine, NACWPI Journal, Down Beat and Modern Drummer are further sources of much value.

As the field of ethnomusicology is developed in higher education, a body of literature is appearing that describes music and instruments of peoples around the world. The Garland World Music series is a good example, as are some publications of the University of Chicago Press.

An interesting dilemma of the present society is keeping the traditional musics, while encompassing new musics. The Indians and Hmong of central Wisconsin are examples of this, with their traditions being surrounded by modern approaches. Some of the traditions are oral rather than written, and are thus subject to a variety of reception by different populations.

It is true, however, that music is an important part of these ethnic groups, and percussion is at the heart of their music. The passing of melodies, harmonies and rhythms from generation to generation is crucial for the permanence of traditional musics. One suspects that native talent occurs generally in any population, regardless of educational attainment. Recording is thus of utmost importance for the notation of music history.

Acoustics

Moore, James L. Acoustics of Bar Percussion Instruments. Columbus, Ohio: Per-Mus Publications, 1978.

The scientific consideration of music can be found in the history of ancient Greece. Indeed, the mathematical work of Pythagoras in the 6th Century B.C., preceded the research of Ptolemy, an astronomer in the 2nd Century A.D. Scholars of that era viewed the harmony of the spheres as rather comparable with harmony in music, something that could be studied and specified. In the 20th Century, music added electronics and the computer into its realm.

Dr. J.L. Moore, a scholar at Ohio State University, wrote the above listed-work during doctoral study in music theory, and offers it for purchase through his publishing company. Dr. Moore's background includes study at the University of Michigan, and performance in percussion with the Indianapolis Symphony and the Columbus Symphony Orchestra, as well as the Brass Band of Columbus. He also taught at Butler University and at the U.S. Navy School of Music. He is a founding editor of Percussive Notes with work in composition.

The four percussion instruments studied in the 1978 publication include marimba, orchestra bells, vibraphone and xylophone. The four instruments were struck mechanically with various mallets. Synthetic keys on the instruments were not a consideration at the time of the research, with content of the bars being the traditional rosewood, steel and aluminum alloy.

The book lists the makeup of the bars, for example, iron, copper, silicon and zinc, depending upon the specific object studied. Modes of vibration were measured, using a stroboscope and oscilloscope to obtain objective information and comparisons.

Literature that was consulted for the study included the works of Chiadni, Helmholtz, Hindemith, Mersenne and Rameau. Other sources included Baldwin, Levarie and Levy.

Factors taken into consideration included the resonators, mallets and ranges of the instruments. Steady state and transient measurements were a part of the experimental work. Modes of vibration among the various instruments were studied and compared. The book's conclusions are intelligent, based upon scientific approaches to the study of acoustics.

Article References

In the particular field of percussion music, this author has written articles for publication beginning with the fall, 1966, issue of <u>Percussive Notes</u>, through the September, 2000, issue of <u>Percussion News</u>, where an etude titled "Timpani Metric Modulation" appears. This piece can be heard over the internet, published by the international Percussive Arts Society that is located in Lawton, Oklahoma.

One source that is in research libraries regarding this kind of writing is the <u>Music Article Guide</u>. The author recalls looking at this reference source in Sibley Music Library at the Eastman School of Music of the University of Rochester in the 1960s as a graduate student working toward a degree in performance and literature.

In the 1990s, the author has found this source at universities in Wisconsin. Examples are Mills Music Library at the University of Wisconsin in Madison, the University Library in the Learning Resources Center on campus of the University of Wisconsin in Stevens Point, the main library at the University of Wisconsin in Eau Claire, and the main library at the University of Wisconsin in Green Bay. Following is a bibliographic listing of the author's references found in <u>Music Article Guide</u> from the 1967-1968 edition through the 1995 edition. This can give the reader an idea of where one may find sources on percussion music, including associated information that can be enlightening and important. As in the standard bibliographic entry, the title of the publication is followed by its volume in Roman numerals, its edition number in Arabic numbers, the season and year(s) in parentheses, and relevant page numbers in that particular issue.

<u>Music Article Guide</u> 111/1 (Winter 1967-68), 30, 39.
<u>Music Article Guide</u> IV/1 (Winter 1968-69), 12, 25, 28, 32.
<u>Music Article Guide</u> IX/1 (Winter 1973-74), 16, 19.
<u>Music Article Guide</u> IX/2 (Spring 1974), 15, 17.
<u>Music Article Guide</u> IX/4 (Fall 1974), 11, 13.
<u>Music Article Guide</u> X/1 (Winter 1974-75), 21, 36.

Music Article Guide XI/2 (Spring 1976), 12, 14.
Music Article Guide XI/3 (Summer 1976), 14, 27.
Music Article Guide XVII/2 (Spring 1982), 6, 11.
Music Article Guide XIX/3 (Summer 1984), 11.
Music Article Guide XX/4 (Fall 1985), 11, 22.
Music Article Guide XXI/1 (Winter 1985-86), 11, 24.
Music Article Guide XXI/2 (Spring 1986), 11, 22.
Music Article Guide XXII/1 (Winter 1986-87), 7, 13.
Music Article Guide XXII/3 (Summer 1987), 12.
Music Article Guide XXI-XXIII (1986-88), 74, 153, 165, 310.
Music Article Guide XXIV/1 (Winter 1988-89), iv, 11.
Music Article Guide XXIV/1-4 (1989), 53, 61.
Music Article Guide XXV1/1 (Winter 1990-91), iv, 6.
Music Article Guide XXVI/3 (Summer 1991), iv, 25.
Music Article Guide XXVI/1-4 (1991), 31, 62, 63, 119.
Music Article Guide XXX/1-4- (1995), 54.

It is noted from the preceding bibliographic list that page numbers in small case Roman numerals are front matter and Arabic numbers are in the main body of the book. Capital letter Roman numerals are volume numbers. This list gives the reader an idea of general activity in the publication of articles on percussion music during the latter half of the 20th Century in the United States.

Articles

Following is a bibliographic essay on articles that the author has written for publication from 1966 to 1998. During that time, the author taught several places, performed in various orchestras and bands, and wrote three books.

Subjects of these articles embrace percussion music from several points of view. Format will be a bibliographic entry for each article, followed by a short summary of the article's content.

It is hoped that the reader will notice several aspects of percussion, even a number of writing styles. A number of editors helped with these publications, and their assistance is much appreciated.

Larrick, Geary. "A Drummer's View of 1984." Faculty Forum 1/3 (April 1979), 3. This was published at the University of Wisconsin-Stevens Point. Headings include Communication, Social Change and Technical Invention. The author discusses important facets of the music world, midway through the second half of the 20th Century.

Larrick, Geary H. "A Study of the Timpani Parts of Beethoven's Symphonies, Part I." National Association of College Wind and Percussion Instructors (NACWPI) Journal XXXIII/3 (Spring 1985), 4. The introduction to this major document was started in the library at the College of Music at the University of Colorado in Boulder, while the remainder of the paper was written in Stevens Point, Wisconsin. Part I deals with the first three of Beethoven's symphonies. Fortunately, the author was able to conduct the First Symphony with the Stevens Point Symphony Orchestra in Michelsen Hall in the Fine Arts Center, as well as the first movement of the Third Symphony. This experience gave the author yet another perspective on the works. Also, the violin part to sections of the Second Symphony was practiced many times on marimba as a student in the School of Music at The Ohio State University.

Larrick, Geary H. University of Wisconsin-Stevens Point. "A Study of the Timpani Parts of Beethoven's Symphonies, Part II." NACWPI Journal XXXIII/4

(Summer 1985), 13. This article discusses the Fourth, Fifth and Sixth Symphonies of Beethoven. Comments include analysis, pedagogy and performance. Music examples are extracted in hand manuscript. The author had conducted the Finale to the Fifth, in arrangement, with the Cambridge, Ohio, High School Orchestra in a performance in the Little Theater at the high school building on Clairmont Avenue. The entire Fifth was studied and conducted with two pianos in the Annex of the Eastman School of Music in a graduate conducting class. The works were also studied in literature classes at the Eastman School and at the University of Colorado.

Larrick, Geary H. "A Study of the Timpani Parts of Beethoven's Symphonies, Part III." NACWPI Journal XXXIV/1 (Fall 1985), 12. Typist for this major document in Stevens Point was the author's wife, Lydia Fang Larrick, a social worker in the Health and Human Services Department for Portage County, with a Bachelor's from the University of Wisconsin-Stevens Point transferred from Edgewood College in Madison, and a Master's from Minnesota State University, Mankato. This lengthy-article includes a bibliography, an appendix, music examples and footnote. It covers the Seventh, Eighth and Ninth Symphonies of the well-known composer. As a performer, the author had the pleasure of performing these works in concert. The Seventh was performed on timpani in the Summer Orchestra at the University of Colorado, while the Eighth was performed on timpani with the Central Wisconsin Symphony Orchestra. The Ninth was performed on cymbals at the Eastman School of Music, and on bass drum with conductor Eric Townell and the Central Wisconsin Symphony Orchestra in Sentry Theater in Stevens Point.

Larrick, Geary, DMA. "Addendum." NACWPI Journal XXXV/1 (Fall 1986), 38. This brief note was the result of a letter that the author received from former Philadelphia Orchestra timpanist Fred Hinger. The letter cleared up some confusion about terminology in pedagogy that was appreciated. Mr. Hinger also played timpani in the orchestra for the Metropolitan Opera in New York City, and taught at the Manhattan School of Music. The author had met Mr. Hinger in Aspen, Colorado, one summer. Hinger's timpani repertoire guidebooks are an important addition to the literature about percussion.

Larrick, Geary. "Analysis of Percussion Music." NACWPI Journal XXXVIII/4 (Summer 1990), 13. This article's reference list includes publications, written by James Blades, Richard Gipson, Jan LaRue, Donald Francis Tovey and the author. The article is concise, bringing out important points with regard to looking at percussion music and making informed decisions about its content. A letter from Professor LaRue motivated the author to pursue the subject, soon after the publication in New York City of the author's first book entitled <u>Analytical and Biographical Writings in Percussion Music</u> (P. Lang).

Larrick, Geary H. "Biography and Analysis of Bob Becker's 'Lahara'." <u>NACWPI Journal</u> XXXIV/4 (Summer 1986), 26. This paper was written at the College of Music at the University of Colorado, with the help of Dr. William Kearns, a horn player and musicologist with special interests in American music. The subject, Bob Becker, was a classmate of the author at the Eastman School of Music, performing together in the Eastman Percussion Ensemble, the Eastman Philharmonia, the Eastman Wind Ensemble and the Rochester Philharmonic Orchestra. The author performed "Lahara" in Boulder and Stevens Point. This essay cites several types of tabla composition, such as Bhumika, Theka, Ti Hai, Rela and Paran. The author has since watched Mr. Becker perform with Nexus at the University of Tennessee, and met him at conferences in Eau Claire and Madison. Becker's composition "Cymbal" is another interesting work of creative art.

Larrick, Geary, DMA. "Black Musicians in History." <u>Multicultural Affairs News</u> 3/2 (Winter 1997), 4. The University of Wisconsin-Stevens Point. This article cites several musicians of the 20th Century, as well as publications and songs. Especially pertinent is the information about the use of this music for practice.

Larrick, Geary. "Chopin for Drums." <u>GP Light</u> 57 (January 1998), 9. The acronymn "GP" in this case stands for Gwiazda Polarna, the name of a Polish newspaper published in Stevens Point, Wisconsin, USA. This article discusses the practice of playing music composed by the 19th Century pianist Chopin on the keyboard percussion such as vibes and marimba or xylophone. It includes a photo of the author in 1957, performing in recital in Ohio on vibraharp.

Larrick, Geary. "Chopin's Minute Waltz." <u>GP Light</u> 77 (September 1999), 4. This article for the English language Polish newspaper published in Stevens Point, is subtitled "What one can do in sixty seconds or so." The point is made the beauty in Chopin's music can be expressed, regardless of duration.

Larrick, Geary H. "Compilation of Published Percussion Ensembles and Percussion with Other Instruments." NACWPI Bulletin XVII/2 (Winter 1968), 16. This lengthy article is introduced by Professor John H. Beck, teacher at the Eastman School of Music in Rochester, New York. The author typed this article's manuscript at Plymouth Avenue South in Rochester, across from the police station. Most of the research was aided by mail delivery.

Larrick, Geary. "Drumming and Fifing of the Civil War." NACWPI Journal XXXVII/1 (Fall 1988), 8. This paper was prepared at the University of Colorado in 1983, as a lecture recital for which the author played the snare drum, accompanied by a flutist. The recital was later presented in the Fine Arts Center at the University of Wisconsin-Stevens Point as part of a lecture series. The paper was presented without performance in 1987 at a Percussive Arts Society International Convention in Saint Louis, Missouri.

Larrick, Geary. "Elliott Carter and His Timpani Pieces." NACWPI Journal XXXVI/2 (Winter 1987-1988), 22. This article on the well known Timpani Pieces includes music examples and bibliography. The author was fortunate in being able to perform four of the Pieces in recital, perhaps giving a fresh look at this music.

Larrick, Geary. "Gorecki Gets 90 Pages in the Musical Quarterly." GP Light 69 (January 1999), 11.

This review was published in an English language Polish newspaper from Stevens Point, Wisconsin. Soloists mentioned include Theresa Erba and Dawn Upshaw.

Larrick, Geary. "Milhaud's Concerto for Percussion--Analysis and Performance, Part 1." The School Musician, Director and Teacher (February 1974), 8. "Part 2," (April 1974), 14. The editor of these two articles was Dr. John Baldwin, a colleague who attended the author's recitals in Stevens Point, Wisconsin, in Old Main Auditorium, and in Boulder, Colorado, in the College of Music Recital Hall. This Concerto is famous among percussionists. It is enjoyable to perform, and interesting to study. Professor Frank Baird assisted in the original preparation of the paper.

Larrick, Geary. "Multicultural Music: Bob Becker's 'Lahara'." NACWPI Journal XXXIX/1 (Fall 1990), 10. This paper was delivered at a conference in Toronto for the Sonneck Society for American Music. At the conference, the author performed snare drum in the Brass Band, and attended a concert of the

Toronto Symphony, writing a positive review that was published in a Sonneck Society publication. In 1990, the term "multicultural" was coming into wider use. In this instance, it refers to the combination of Asian tabla drum ideas and American drum audiments.

Larrick, Geary. "Music for Keyboard Percussion." <u>NACWPI Journal</u> (Fall 1998), 18. At the time of the publication of this article, the author resided in Plover in central Wisconsin. The article speaks about arrangements published earlier in the century by well-known percussionists George Hamilton Green and Clair Omar Musser. The article's reference list includes recent scholarship on the 19th Century pianist Chopin.

The term "keyboard percussion" refers to the instruments that have a keyboard arranged like the piano and is struck with mallets. Specifically, instruments include the glockenspiel, orchestra bells, marimba, vibraphone and xylophone. A generic term for these instruments is "xylophone." Another general term that is sometimes used is "mallets" or "mallet instruments." Around the third quarter of the 20th Century, the term "bar instruments" was also used. Actually, the ethnic xylophone that is graduated in sound but not tuned like the piano, is technically a keyboard percussion instrument, too. Just yesterday (September 13, 2000), the author heard and saw one of these played on campus.

Tuning and timbre were very alike, however. Interestingly, the player of the newer model had the keyboard arranged with the larger keys to the player's right, placing the higher sounds toward the left. This arrangement of pitches ranging from high to low, left to right, is the same as the German arrangement of timpani traditionally. Most American timpanists place the larger, lower sounding drum to the player's left, and the higher to the right. The German style, however, is to place the lower drum ;o the right and the higher drum to the left. This is the style used by the keyboard percussion player seen yesterday. The playing was quite good, without question.

Bach Two-part Inventions work well with two players on two marimbas. The music is substantive, tonal, scalar and at times contrapuntal. Likewise, Mozart flute and violin concertos have a solo part that can be played on the marimba. This would acquaint the college student with important music within a Western heritage. Of course, the xylophone has a long history in Eastern musics. The gamelan of Indonesia has bronze xylophones that are beautiful.

17

Modern marimba concertos like those by Creston, Kurka, Milhaud, Basta and Rosauro are important recent additions to the keyboard percussion repertoire. Indeed, the Golden Age of Percussion may live on into the 21st Century. Emphases now include ethnomusicology, popular musics and jazz, in addition to the traditional study of Western tonal music from the Middle Ages to the 20th Century.

Larrick, Geary. "On Musical Ability, Conducting and Analysis." NACWPI Journal XXXVII/3 (Spring 1989), 29. Editor for this and the other NACWPI articles was Dr. Richard Weerts, a music professor at Truman State University in Kirksville, Missouri. The National Association of College Wind and Percussion Instructors is connected with the Music Educators National Conference. The organization promotes high quality playing and teaching, composition and a studied approach toward pedagogy of the wind and percussion instruments in higher education.

. This article, though philosophical in nature, relates experiences that the author learned from teaching at levels including preschool through university. A special effort is made to promote interdisciplinary considerations of college faculty in music, to the extent where they can overlap and benefit the student. Conducting is here included as musical performance.

A pitch is made for the conductor of an ensemble to practice analytical skills in preparation of the score before rehearsal. The result is an informed idea about the music, and therefore a more responsible performance. Musical ability is touched upon in a theoretical manner.

Larrick, Geary. "Paul Creston and His Marimba Concerto." NACWPI Journal XXXV111/1 (Fall 1989), 9. This paper was delivered to an American music conference at the University of Missouri - Kansas City earlier in the year of publication. The author had performed the Creston concerto in recital in Colorado, and had talked about the work with Charles Owen in Aspen after he had recorded the first movement with the Philadelphia Orchestra. The original research was done in Boulder in summer, 1975, with Professor Charles Eakin. Previously the author had used the first movement as an audition piece with success near Washington, D.C., for The United States Army Band. The concerto was also used in teaching with advanced students at the University of Wisconsin - Stevens Point. An analysis by the author was also published in spring, 1989, in the book entitled <u>Analytical and Biographical Writings in Percussion Music</u>, published in New York City by Peter Lang Publishing.

Larrick, Geary. "Percussion References in the Bible." <u>Percussive Notes</u> 29/6 (August 1991), 56. This article is part of a Focus on Research column, edited by Richard Gipson and James Lambert. The original work appeared in this author's book entitled <u>Musical References and Song Texts in the Bible</u>, published in 1990 by The Edwin Mellen Press in Lewiston, New York. Assistance with preparation of the manuscript was given by Dr. Richard Pinnell, chair for the Department of Music at the University of Wisconsin in La Crosse. Other assistance was given by professors at Edgewood College in Madison, Wisconsin. The percussion part of the book, excerpted in <u>Percussive Notes</u>, was actually the start of the research, then study of the other instruments followed. Important work was done with a large concordance in the library of Saint Paul's United Methodist Church in Stevens Point, Wisconsin. A diaconal minister in Milwaukee guided the author toward the eventual publisher in western New York. The book is included in the 2000 <u>Whitaker's Books in Print</u>, and in <u>Books in Print 1999-2000</u>.

Larrick, Geary. "Poem for the Viola." <u>Barney Street</u> (1997), 46. Editor of this publication from the University of Wisconsin-Stevens Point was M.M. Camps. The piece, with musical typescript by Donald Jones, was originally published by G and L Publishing in Stevens Point. It has been performed on viola in the Philadelphia, Pennsylvania, area, and on piano by the composer for a general music class at P.J. Jacobs Junior High School in Stevens Point. The 1997 publication includes music notation without commentary. The original Poem was expanded to include percussion as a duo piece of music. In the school performance, the author/composer read a poem by a famous poet to accompany the presentation. The two poems, one literary and one musical, were warmly received by the audience. The author later performed the Poem on marimba for school programs and Community Access Television in Stevens Point. The music's alto clef gives the reader food for thought, as it is said. The basic idea of the Poem was associated with romantic tone poems for orchestra that the author had heard or performed in the past. It is effective as a practice piece as well as for performance.

Larrick, Geary. "Proper Angklung Technique." <u>Percussive Notes</u> 28/3 (Spring 1990), 59. As this segment is being written, the Percussive Arts Society is preparing past issues of this publication for availability online for members. The illustration for this article was drawn by the author's son, Scott Turner (Larrick) Tielens, when he was a high school student in suburban Saint Louis, although the project was begun in Stevens Point. The instruments photographed were part of a collection owned by Reverend C.H. Fang in Stevens Point.

Larrick, Geary. "Social Science and Multicultural Music." The Small City and Regional Community 13 (1998), edited by E.J. Miller and R.P. Wolensky. Stevens Point: Foundation Press ISBN 0-932310-40-0, 315. This paper was presented at the University of Wisconsin-Stevens Point in the University Center. The presentation also included the author performing an original composition titled "Repertory List II," with audio tape and tambourine. Multidisciplinary considerations like the combination of music and science are an interesting intellectual approach. The practice of medicine has been called both an art and a science, and likewise, music can be looked at from the points of view of both art and science. Presently, the scientific part would involve the computer and the synthesizer, as well as the study of acoustics in its several parameters. Indeed, the practicing musician needs to look at his or her art not only from the standpoint of artistic expression in musical values, but also from the standpoint of practical acoustics. In the author's one hundred plus music compositions since 1967, an important problem to be solved is the consideration of sound sources, production of volume or loudness, and contrast in dynamics. This author's preference is for a classical approach to dynamics, that is, a minimum of sudden contrasts in the music. A thread of idea that continues throughout the piece can perhaps best be expressed in a moderate approach to dynamics, rather than in episodic explosions of sound. This is in line historically, since the 19th Century was more of a romantic period in the western world, and the 20th Century in classical music can be viewed as more of a classic period. The addition of science to music in the 20th Century gives a rather objective approach, in contrast to past subjective approaches. In the last decade of the century, multiculturalism in music is seen as a result of air travel and cross communication between cultures worldwide, that did not exist on that level previously. Certainly the growth of the discipline of ethnomusicology in this period has helped to add to one's knowledge and understanding of peoples and music.

Larrick, Geary. "Symphonic Percussion: Metric Modulation." Percussive Notes 27/1 (Fall 1988), 46. This article is part of the Focus on Performance column, edited by Michael Rosen and Richard Weiner. It includes a bibliography, music examples and original exercises. A follow-up etude titled "Timpani Metric Modulation," appears in the September, 2000, Percussion News, and can be heard over the internet. Both publications are produced by the Percussive Arts Society, Lawton, Oklahoma.

Larrick, Geary H. "Toward A Musical Percussionist." Percussive Notes 5/1 (Fall 1966), 3. Editor of this first published article by the author was James L. Moore, the percussion instructor at Ohio State. The paper was written the previous summer when the author was teaching at Foster Music Camp on the campus of Eastern Kentucky University in Richmond. It gives an overview of contemporary literature. Pedagogically, the article promotes what later became known as "total percussion," meaning not only drumming but also keyboard percussion and timpani in one's study. In the year 2000, this translates to the beginning percussion student becoming acquainted with drum and bells, when that is practical. There will always be specialists and personal preferences. For example, one person may have a special love for playing the marimba. However, in percussion education it is recommended generally that students pursue learning about not only drums, but also keyboard percussion and timpani. The drum set can be an effective outlet for some students, and it is popular in numerous music groups outside of schools. The values of music learned in a school can certainly be transferred to popular music and jazz, in a more relaxed situation. Another avenue of approach, also, is performance in church environments. These can be a rich playground for the dedicated musician in devotion.

Larrick, Geary. "Two Contemporary Composers." GP Light 54 (October 1997), 8. This is the author's first article in central Wisconsin's production of an English language Polish newspaper. The subjects are K. Penderecki and M. Ptaszynska. The author was part of the percussion section of the Eastman Wind Ensemble in 1969 when that group recorded Penderecki's "Pittsburgh Overture" in the Eastman Theatre, in Rochester, New York. The music was an interesting challenge, with its chance or aleatoric elements, and many timpani. The author was thus inspired to compose, years later, a "Trio Sonata" for twelve timpani, three players. This chamber piece received a positive review nationally written by a Texas percussion professor and performer.

M. Ptaszynska, also born in Poland, is known for her original compositions and master classes taught in the United States. She was also important in helping to establish modern percussion in Poland in the 20th Century. She teaches at the University of Chicago.

In summary, these several articles give an overview to the reader of subjects touched upon in percussion from 1966 to 2000. There are probably a few, or perhaps several, threads of idea that run through each article, then get developed in later work. This does not discount the early work, however, for at times it is not only interesting but also enlightening to consider older ideas in perspective.

Articles Reference

Diamond, Harold J. Music Analyses. New York: Schirmer Books, 1991.

Larrick, Geary H. "Eight Pieces for Four Timpani by Elliott Carter," 180.

Larrick, Geary. "Milhaud's Concerto for Percussion, " 361. -

This reference book compiled by Harold J. Diamond includes information about many sources, including the two written by this author listed herewith. Published in New York City in 1991, the volume is well written.

The Timpani Pieces composed by Elliott Carter are well known among professional percussionists. There are eight, as the title of Carter's booklet implies, with a suggestion that four may be chosen for any singular presentation.

In the early 1970s, this author prepared four of the Timpani Pieces for a doctoral recital at the University of Colorado in Boulder. Performance was on four Rogers timpani in the recital hail at the College of Music. A reprise presentation was made, also on Rogers timpani, in Michelsen Concert Hall in the Fine Arts Center at the University of Wisconsin-Stevens Point. As a faculty member at UWSP, the author guided a student performance of one of the Pieces on a traditional Wednesday afternoon recital program of college student performers.

It is interesting to perform a piece of music, then to listen to it from the audience. Further, the author wrote a paper on the Timpani Pieces that was eventually published. Approach to the analysis was descriptive, looking at different areas. This concept was chosen since percussion as serious art music for solo instruments is a rather new phenomenon of the middle 20th Century. Thus, the idiom was somewhat unfamiliar and in need of accurate description, based upon new concepts for composition within a new medium of percussion.

A master composer like Carter solved well the inherent challenges of percussion notation. This music with a western tradition speaks in a contemporary language that expresses universally. In other words, a listener in Malaysia should have no difficulty understanding the art, in comparison with a listener in New

23

York where the music originated. Conversely, an American may find to be interesting music produced in Asia, with a certain degree of appreciation.

This is the beauty of music as communication: it can express adequately, regardless of cultural heritage. Its aesthetic is important.

Darius Milhaud's featured piece for percussion and small orchestra was a groundbreaking work in the early part of the 20th Century. The author was lucky to be able to perform the Concerto with wind ensemble accompaniment at the University of Colorado, then to perform the work with two pianists accompanying at the University of Wisconsin-Stevens Point, and to conduct the Concerto with the Stevens Point Symphony Orchestra, collaborating with a featured student soloist. Indeed, the president of the orchestra's board of directors told me after the concert that he believed that the Milhaud Concerto for Percussion with Small Orchestra was perfectly suited for an ensemble such as ours.

The author wrote papers on the Concerto in Colorado, and they were eventually published. As a concert listener, the author was pleased to view a Concerto performance by Professor James Latimer from the University of Wisconsin in Madison, performing with the Racine Symphony Orchestra in southeastern Wisconsin.

Another interesting percussion part written by Darius Milhaud is the multipercussion music for "La Creation du Monde." This was published in 1929 in Paris by Editions Max Eschiq, later distributed in the United States of America by Associated Music Publishers. The percussion ("batterie") part of La Creation is notated in single and double staves variously, beginning with bass drum having the cymbal detached. Other drums are part of the collection, as well as blocks of metal and wood. The La Creation percussion part is published in clear notation in Albert Payson's fine book, "The Snare Drum in the Concert Hall," that Payson published himself in suburban Chicago with the firm Payson Percussion Products. Mr. Payson played with the Chicago Symphony.

As an undergraduate percussion music education student at The Ohio State University, it was this author's pleasure to read through one of the jury pieces for percussion that was produced by the Paris Conservatory. This multipercussion work with piano accompaniment, helped to acquaint the author, who has French heritage, with contemporary French arpproaches to percussion music. Thus Milhaud's La Creation batterie part is not only interesting, but also rather familiar.

24

The batterie part displays an occasional accent mark, though of course the artist percussionist will add phrase ideas to his or her percussion performance above and beyond that printed in the music. Drum rolls are notated with a tremolo sign, a sound similar to that produced on the early vibraphones with sustaining pedal and moving discs.

Dynamic range in the batterie part ranges loud to soft, with extremes at both ends of the continuum notated well. At times one hand will play one dynamic, while the other hand plays a different dynamic level. For example, the right hand may play medium loud while the left hand plays medium soft. This is similar to piano technique, when the player wants to emphasize a right hand melody while playing a left hand accompaniment of harmony.

The bass drum is played with a pedal in a concert situation, comparing with the standard drum set that is used in jazz and popular musics. As with Carter's music, the master composer Milhaud solved many challenges in regard to notation of percussion. Directions are in French, requiring the performer to become acquainted with that language insofar as percussion is concerned. A very important aid for the performing percussionist, of course, is owning a small dictionary that translates foreign terms.

In summary, the two compositions cited in Diamond's fine book , having to do with percussion and this author, have a very strong background. The works have heritage, influences from both the past and the present, with an eye open to the future. The music in this case was written by 1965, published about in 1991, and is important in 2000. The history of western music, then, is of most importance in the scheme of percussion pedagogy. A general volume like The Enjoyment of Music written by Joseph Machlis (New York: W.W. Norton, 1963), is recommended to the reader to offer perspective to the Carter and Milhaud compositions.

Audio Recording Review

<u>Midwest Jazz Masters</u>. Ellis and Peterson and Rhyne. Minneapolis, Minnesota: Arts Midwest, 1997.

Executive producer for this excellent recording is Dawn Renee Jones. Featured soloists are Manty Ellis, guitar, Milwaukee; Jeanne Arland Peterson, piano/vocals, Minneapolis; Melvin Rhyne, organ/piano, Milwaukee. These three musicians display a wealth of experience, articulation, technique, ability, knowledge, musicianship and expertise with their instruments.

Composers represented on this very fine album include Carey, Dubin, Ellis, Gershwin, Higgenbotham, Martin, Mercer, Montgomery, Rome and Warren. Titles include "From Moment to Moment," "Hi-Heel Sneakers," "Just As Though You Were Here," "I Like You," "I Only Have Eyes for You," "Summertime," "Trane Stop," "Why Did I Choose You" and "You've Changed." Melodic improvisation is at a professional level, and rhythmic movement develops well over a solid foundation.

Supporting personnel on this technologically good recording include B. Allard, violin; B. Berg, drums; J. Cuneo, violin; C. Daws, violin; H. Daws, violin; G. Hughes, drums; D. Karr, flute; B. Peterson, bass; W. Pickens, piano; R. Teco, violin; K. Washington, drums; and J. Whitfield, bass. Musicality, balance, dynamics, enesmble cohesiveness and interpretation are excellent. The experience of the featured soloists is notable.

Repetition and variety are well balanced on this important recording publication. Sound and tone are pleasant: this is definitely music for all seasons.

The art of jazz began in the United States, but has roots in Africa and the Americas. Your attention is directed toward a booklet published by G and L Publishing of Stevens Point, Wisconsin, entitled <u>A Selected Bibliography for Jazz Music</u>. The co-authors are Richard Pinnell and Geary Larrick. The publication was presented in article form in a journal published in Seoul, Korea, entitled <u>Currents in Musical Thought</u>. Also, the Jazz Music Bibliography was reviewed in an Arts Midwest newsletter. The Bibliography is not comprehensive, but rather is concise, organized and enlightening. Both authors have performed jazz together and in other groups, and both have doctorates in music.

Attention is also directed toward important jazz music programs at the University of North Texas, the Berklee College of Music in Boston, and programs at Ohio State, University of Wisconsin at Eau Claire and Stevens Point, in particular. Jazz is practiced worldwide, however.

Bibliography on Native American Topics

The scholarly study of Native American history is now a popular area of endeavour. The subject includes not only history, but also culture and art. Following is an introduction to this important subject.

Abrams, Robert. "The Beat of the Drum: What Does the Fetus Hear?" Percussive Notes 37/3 (June 1999), 62.

Berner, Robert L. Defining American Indian Literature. Lewiston: Edwin Mellen, 1999.

Isernhagen, Hartwig. Momaday, Vizenor, Armstrong: Conversations on American Indian Writing. Norman: University of Oklahoma Press, 1999.

Korp, Maureen. The Sacred Geography of the American Mound-Builders. Lewiston: Edwin Mellen, 1990.

Larrick, Geary. Ode To A Menominee. Stevens Point: G and L Publishing, 1985.

MultiCultural Review. Westport, Connecticut: Greenwood Publishing Group, 2000.

TeCube, Leroy. Year in Nam: A Native American Soldier's Story. Lincoln: University of Nebraska Press, 1999.

The reader is guided to bookstores, also, where are many new publications. Native American history is important, timely and interesting. New, innovative work is needed in this field.

Black History

February is Black History Month in the United States. In 1990, this author was doing research for a book that was published in 1992 by The Edwin Mellen Press in Lewiston, New York. Title of the book is <u>Biographical Essays on Twentieth-Century Percussionists</u>. The volume contains several sketches on African-American percussionists.

A paper was drawn up extracting the information about these nine musicians, and was read during Black History Month in the University Center at the University of Wisconsin-Stevens Point. Subjects are Art Blakey, Jack DeJohnette, Lionel Hampton, Bobby Hutcherson, Milt Jackson, Elayne Jones, James Latimer, Harvey Mason and Max Roach.

The research paper became an article in the National Association of College Wind and Percussion Instructors <u>(NACWPI) Journal</u>, appearing in 1997. This article is referenced in the Repertoire International de Litterature Musicale (RILM) <u>Abstracts</u>, and in <u>The Music Index</u>. The book is referenced in Books in Print and Whitaker's.

Some of the material was rewritten to be included in an essay titled "20th Century African-American Percussionists," that appears in the author's book published in 1999 entitled <u>Bibliography, History, Pedagogy and Philosophy in Music and Percussion</u>. The publisher is again The Edwin Mellen Press in Lewiston, New York. This essay is included in the volume's third section subtitled Scholarship in Music.

The 1999 book with ISBN number 0-7734-8165-6, is volume sixty-two in the publisher's continuing series Studies in the History and Interpretation of Music. This book is referenced in <u>Books in Print 1999-2000</u>.

It is indeed rewarding for an author to be able to sustain a single project such as this one for an entire decade. As a lifetime listener and practitioner of music, the author has been more or less acquainted with the work of these excellent musicians for some time. The artists are well recorded on disc and in print. Thus there is much material available in publication that well represents their exceptional talent and work. A recent listening experience included the recording <u>Jazz-A-Live</u> with Lionel Hampton, published in Canada.

Books Reference

Books in Print 1999-2000. New Providence, New Jersey: R.R. Bowker, 1999. Volume 3, Authors, page 5651.

Larrick, Geary. Analytical and Biographical Writings in Percussion Music.

Larrick, Geary. Bibliography, History, Pedagogy and Philosophy in Music and Percussion.

Larrick, Geary. Biographical Essays on Twentieth-Century Percussionists.

Larrick, Geary. Musical References and Song Texts in the Bible.

These four books, published in New York from 1989 to 1999, constitute a significant amount of scholarly material with an emphasis on percussion music. Collaborating artists were Professor Herbert Sandmann, Lydia Fang Larrick and music typist Donald Jones.

Various subjects are discussed within the more than eight hundred pages. Topics include Beethoven symphonies, and percussion music composed by Carter, Milhaud, Burton, Cahn, Becker, Brown, Dahi, Creston. Professional biographical subjects include Beck, Abe, Pustjens, Chenoweth, Ptaszynska, Street, Moore, Smith, Small, Ludwig, Dash and Payson, among others.

Building

The small child enjoys building things. Of course, the adult typically enjoys a similar activity. The following review covers this subject rather carefully.

Hopkin, Bart. Musical Instrument Design. Tucson, Arizona: See Sharp Press, 1996. ISBN 1-884365-08-6, 181 pages, softcover, $18.95. Introduction by Jon Scoville.

This fascinating volume includes an annotated bibliography, a detailed index and helpful illustrations. Writing style effectively bridges the scholarly and the technical with defined terminology.

Subtitle for this very good book is "Practical Information for Instrument Design." Bart Hopkin has composed, performed guitar, researched and taught. He is a graduate of Harvard and San Francisco State, and has been the editor of the quarterly journal Experimental Musical Instruments since 1985. This book's cover photography exhibits a glass marimba, gourd drums and an unusual bell horn.

Besides a useful glossary, the text contains four appendices on tools and materials, frequency and tuning charts, amplification and additional information about air columns, toneholes and woodwind keying mechanisms.

Chapters on aerophones, chordophones, idiophones and membranophones offer much technical information written in an understandable manner. Some of the terminology relates back to the well known German musicologist K. Sachs.

Musical Instrument Design contains much scientific information, along with recommendations and suggestions regarding instrument construction. Many ideas and instruments are discussed, covering the orchestral gamut from strings and winds to percussion and special effects.

Sample chapter subheadings include air columns and chambers, dampers, drum tuning, mallets and sticks, modes of vibration, pitch control for wind instruments, resonance, reverberation and sympathetic vibration, scrapers, sirens, string instrument forms, tuning forks and tuning systems. In addition, there are several generally short passages on specific topics such as "A Basic End-struck Percussion-tubes Set," "Locating String Stopping Point,," "Making A Scraper Flute," "Making A Tuned Gong Set," "Making Single Reed Mouthpieces," "String Materials" and "Strings with Tuned Air Resonators." Several of the essays incorporate high quality drawings.

Generally speaking, this good volume incorporates ideas that remind one of the work of Harry Partch. There is a successful combination of the technical and aesthetic.

Business and Music

When the author turned sixteen years of age in Cambridge, Ohio, the local organization of the American Federation of Musicians invited me to join, in 1959. Now, forty years later, the author is a member of the local of the AF of M called Madison Area Musicians Association. Other short tenures were enjoyed in Baltimore, Maryland, and in Rochester, New York, in the 1960s, then in central Wisconsin before consolidation. In high school, the author played vibes in a combo led by a saxophonist whose day job was assistant manager of the local J.C. Penney store. At one of our late night chats following a gig, at a nearby restaurant, the leader brought up the idea that music is business. However, the teenage vibist took the side of the artist, rather than that of a business person.

Now, in the year 2000, the author and others recognize the importance of considering the business side of music. Symphony orchestras must market their product, just as do jazz and popular musicians. Indeed, one of the most interesting aspects of symphonic music in the last decade of the 20th Century, is the founding of a new orchestra based in Kuala Lumpur, Malaysia. It was the author's pleasure to meet with leaders of the Malaysian Philharmonic Orchestra in November, 1997, in Pittsburgh, Pennsylvania, across the street from Heinz Hall, home of the Pittsburgh Symphony Orchestra.

Another exciting growth in symphonic music has been the steady change of the Central Wisconsin Symphony Orchestra. When the author arrived in Stevens Point, Wisconsin, in 1969 from Rochester, New York, the Stevens Point Symphony Orchestra rehearsed and performed in Old Main Building on campus of the Wisconsin State University there. Within a few years, the school was renamed the University of Wisconsin-Stevens Point, and the orchestra gained a broader base.

As music director and conductor of the Stevens Point Symphony Orchestra for a couple of years, the author learned much about symphonic music with a relatively small orchestra, as well as an introduction to the business side of music. Later, as timpanist for the CWSO, the author had the pleasure of performing the orchestral standard repertoire, as well as some modern music. Twenty-five years performing in the ensemble gave the author a lot of good concerts, enjoyable audiences, new perspectives and maturity in technique.

In the year 2000, the freelance musician must combine business and music, just as does the board member of a symphony orchestra or leader of a combo. Likewise, the chair or administrative head of a music department can profit from a rudimentary knowledge of business. Thus, the following list of publications may help the reader in getting an idea of what is involved with the two disciplines. A perusal of these works can hopefully give the reader food for thought, enlightenment and assistance with everyday decisions regarding the two fields.

1902 Edition of the Sears, Roebuck Catalogue. New York: Crown Publishers, 1969.

1996 Wisconsin Business Directory. Omaha, Nebraska: American Business Directories, 1995.

Allen, Bob. "Success: Process or Product?" Percussive Notes 34/2 (April 1996), 55.

Barnhart, Stephen L. Percussionists: A Biographical Dictionary. Westport, Connecticut: Greenwood Press, 2000.

"Business." Webster's New Universal Unabridged Dictionary. Cleveland, Ohio: New.World, 1983.

Denov, Sam. "Employment Classifications." Percussive Notes 38/3 (June 2000), 72.

Kernan, Michael. "The Talking Drums." Smithsonian 31/3 (June 2000), 27.

Kinnard, William N. and Paesani, Judith B. "Business Cycles." Encyclopedia Americana 5 (1994), 45.

Larrick, Geary and Kawles, Terrance. "Music as Business: A Bibliography." NACWPI Journal XLVIII/4 (Summer 2000), 7.

Lesonsky, Rieva. "Better than Ever." Entrepreneur (January 1996), 6.

Markets '92: The Five Year Outlook for the North American Forest Products Industry. San Francisco: Widman Management Consultants, 1992.

Music Industry Directory. Chicago: Marquis, 1983.

Percussion Katalog. Karisruhe, Germany: H. Brandt, 1999.

Pride, William M. and Ferrell, O.C. <u>Marketing</u>. Boston: Houghton Mifflin, 1991.

"Publishers." <u>Books in Print 1996-97</u>, Volume 9. New Providence, New Jersey: R.R. Bowker, 1996.

Randel, Don Michael. <u>Harvard Concise Dictionary of Music</u>. Cambridge, Massachusetts: The Belknap Press of Harvard University Press, 1998.

Steingraber, Fred G. "The New Business Realities of the Twenty-first Century." <u>Business Horizons</u> 39/6 (November 1996), 2.

Stewart, James B. "The World of Business." <u>The New Yorker</u> (November 25, 1996), 78.

Swed, Mark. "The Twentieth-Century: Remembering
Modern Music." <u>The Musical Quarterly</u> 80/1 (Spring 1996), 58.

Children's Literature

Literature on percussion written for children is a fascinating area of study. Recently I went to a public library, and at a computer catalogue keyboard typed in the keyword "drums." The result is a good indication of what is available in the field. The author's daughter had been a regular patron of the public library with her father since infancy, and in the interim I had learned to find holdings via computer.

The result was finding five volumes in the field. In the following bibliography, I have added two of my own related publications. One is an article that reports school youth concerts, and the other is a recent composition that was originally produced for presentation in a preschool at a university.

Subjects addressed include cultural diversity, reading at different levels, photography, construction of instruments, performers, playing technique and rhythm. Publication dates range from 1960 to 1998.

Bailey, Bernadine. Bells, Bells, Bells. New York: Dodd, Mead and Company, 1978.

Kettelkamp, Larry. Drums, Rattles and Bells. USA: William Morrow & Company, 1960.

Larrick, Geary. "The Creative Youth Concert." Brass and Percussion 11/4 (Fall 1974), 12.

Larrick, Geary. Repertory List II. Plover, Wisconsin: G and L Publishing, 1998.

Lillegard, Dee. Percussion. Chicago: Children's Press, 1987.

Price, Christine. Talking Drums of Africa. New York: Charles Scribner's Sons, 1973.

Shipton, Alyn. Exploring Music: Percussion. Austin, Texas: Raintree Steck-Vaughn, 1994.

When the author's daughter was in the second grade, I presented a youth classroom concert in her school. The title of the lecture was on the subject of pen pals, since that was what the class was doing that week. My presentation included my 1992 book and a snare drum. Two subjects were chosen: a pen pal I had gotten to know in Perth, Australia, through the Percussive Arts Society, and the founder of a drum company. I read the two essays, then demonstrated silently a drum produced by that company. Questioners included twins that were friends of my daughters, sitting brilliantly in the front row. Later, in early 1999, I got to meet the son of the drum company founder in Madison, Wisconsin, at a state chapter PAS meeting, when he responded with a comment about the essay I was reading from my 1999 book. In conclusion, it's a small world for both big and little people.

Compact Disc Review

Richeson, Dane Maxim, conductor. <u>Lawrence University Percussion Ensemble</u>. Appleton, Wisconsin: Lawrence University, 1995.

At a jazz concert in Pfiffner Park on the Wisconsin River in Stevens Point, the author heard Professor Richeson play the drum set with a combo. In a brief discussion following the presentation, the percussionist and the author learned of a common interest in the work of the composer A. Ginastera. Then Mr. Richeson gave me a complimentary recording, listed above. This is an example of a typical review that I would write. My reviews have appeared through the years in the <u>NACWPI Journal, 20th Century Music</u> and <u>MultiCultural Review</u>.

Specifically, this high quality recording contains four compositions exceeding twelve minutes each, in duration. Included are "Crown of Thorns" by David Maslanka, "Elective Affinities I" for percussion quartet by Andrew Frank, "Marimba Quartet" in two movements by Daniel Levitan, and "Cantata para America Magica" by Alberto Ginastera (1961). The soprano soloist is Patrice Michaels Bedi, and the cover art is by Joe Fournier.

Numerous drums, idiophones, keyboard percussion, pianos and voice can well be heard in this fine recording of contemporary classical music. The drums are appropriately tuned, so that the difference between melodic and untuned percussion is apparent. Tonal quality of the instruments is excellent. Dynamics range from very soft to quite loud, in a sonorous atmosphere that the percussion ensemble can effectively produce. Timbre and rhythms are well combined. Metrical movement is sophisticated, while melodies are more vertical than linear in nature.

The dramatic soprano part in Ginastera's composition is virtuosic and tastefully done. The vocal text is articulated dramatically, and pitch on the entire recording is very good. Durations and decay of sounds are discernible. Percussive impact is well recorded, not overdone. It is aurally apparent that good choices were made with regard to sticks and mallets.

Music on this educationally produced recording is at times modal, syncopated and grand. Emphasis is upon clear technique, dynamic contrast, intelligent rhythm, tone color and development of idea. Congratulations are due to the performers for this important and enjoyable presentation.

Compilation from 1968

Larrick, Geary H. "Compilation of Published Percussion Ensembles and Percussion with Other Instruments." NACWPI Bulletin XVII/2 (Winter 1968), 16.

This interesting list was drawn up at the request of John H. Beck, percussion instructor at the Eastman School of Music of the University of Rochester, where the author was a graduate assistant. Professor Beck is also timpanist in the Rochester Philharmonic Orchestra, and presided over the international Percussive Arts Society. The article is rewritten here with the kind permission of Dr. Richard Weerts, editor of the NACWPI Journal, the new name of the publication soon after the appearance of this article. A reprint appeared in Percussive Notes, and we have been permitted to rewrite by the Percussive Arts Society.

Sources for this compilation were primarily the contemporary publishers catalogues. It may be interesting to the reader to find out who was writing and publishing, and what were the titles of many works available in 1968.

In the original article, publishers named include American Composers Alliance in New York City, Henry Adler in New York, American Music Edition in New York, Associated Music Publishers in New York, Arizona State University in Tempe, James Basta, Belwin on Long Island, Boosey and Hawkes in New York, Bourne Music Company in New York, Brook Publishing Company in Cleveland Heights in Ohio, Broude Brothers on Long Island, Claude Benny Press, Chance in Austin in Texas, Chappell in New York, M.M. Cole in Chicago, Charles Cohn in New York City. More publishers mentioned in the article include the Fleisher Library in Philadelphia, Sam Fox in New York City, Florida State University in Tallahassee, Kendor Music in Delevan in New York, Robert King in North Easton in Massachusetts, Alphonse Leduc in Paris in France in Europe, Ludwig Drum Company in Chicago, Ludwig Music Publishing in Cleveland, MCA Music in New York, Music For Percussion in New York, Mills Music in

New York, Oxford University Press in New York, C.F. Peters in New York, Percussive Notes in Columbus in Ohio, Percussion Press in Massachusetts.

Other publishers include Theodore Presser in Pennsylvania, Mitchell Peters in Dallas, G. Schirmer in New York City, Slingerland Drum Company in Niles in Illinois, Southern Music Company in San Antonio, Saint Olaf College in Northfield in Minnesota, the University of Michigan in Ann Arbor, and Weintraub in New York City.

Composers included in the 1968 list of percussion with other instruments, are Samuel Adler, Samuel Barber, Bela Bartok, Warren Benson, Philip Bezanson, Paul Bowles, Thomas Brown, Robert Buggert, John Cage, Louis Calabro, Thomas Canning, Barney Childs, Wen-chung Chou, Michael Colgrass.

Others in that list include Aaron Copland, Henry Cowell, John Crawford, Paul Creston, Emma Lou Diemer, Charles Dodge, Richard Donovan, James Drew, Harold Farberman, Vivian Fine, Nicolas Flagello, Edwin Gerschefski, Alberto Ginastera, Peggy Glanville-Hicks, Eugene Glickman, Roger Goeb, David Gordon, James Hanna, Lou Harrison, Herbert Haufrecht, Brent Heisinger, Gustav Holst, Alan Hovhaness, John Huggler, Cole Iverson, M. William Karlins, Ellis Kohs, David Kozinski, William Kraft, Gail Kubik, Robert Kurka, Billy Jim Layton, Ursula Mamlok, Luc-Andre Marcel.

More composers in this category include Jack McKenzie, Darius Milhaud, Edward Jay Miller, Charles Mills, Joshua Missal, James L. Moore, Walter Mourant, Robert Nagel, Vaclav Nelhybel, Lionel Nowak, Hall Overton, Robert Parris, Julia Perry, Daniel Pinkham, Walter Piston, Raoul Pleskow, Sanford H. Reuning, Silvestre Revueltas, Ned Rorem, Jerome Rosen, Marko Rothmuller, Armand Russell, William Russell, Lab Schifrin, Adolph Schreiner, Elna Sherman, Karlheinz Stockhausen, Leon Stein, Alan Stout, Carbos Surinach, Elias Tannenhaum, Clifford Taylor, David A. Tobias, Franz Waxman, Charles Wuorinen, Paul Zonn. Composers of percussion ensemble music from the 1968 article include Alan Abel, George Antheil, Tony Aubin, Jacob Avshalomov, Harry Bartlett, Robert Bauernschmidt, Louis Bellson, Warren Benson, Jerry Bilik, Boris Blacher, Luigi Boccherini, Jacques Bondon, Paul Bonneau, Henry Brant, R.Smith Brindle, Mervin Britton, Wayne Brodkorb, Thomas Brown, Donald Browne, Robert Buggert, John Cage, Lou Harrison, Thomas Canning, Nick Ceroli, Carlos Chavez, Bobby Christian, Owen Clark, Gary Coleman, Michael Colgrass, Henry Cowell, Thomas L. Davis, Serge DeGastyne, William Dorn, Murl Eddy, El-Dabh, Marcel Farago, Harold Farberman, Sandy Feldstein, H.E.

Firestone, Vic Firth, Richard Fitz, Donald K. Gilbert, Alberto Ginastera, Peggy Glanville-Hicks, Saul Goodman, Marty Gold.

More composers of percussion ensembles from the late 1960s include Morton Gould, Phil Grant, Ray Green, Elizabeth Gyring, Rex Hall, Haskell Harr, Haubenstock-Ramati, Alyn Heim, Sidney Hodkinson, Matthew Hopkins, Gordon Jacob, Jacques Dalcroze, Danys Jemison, Donald Jenni, Frederick Karlin, Erich Katz, Robert Kelly, William Kraft, Ernst Krenek, Phillip Lambro, James F. Latimer, Maxine Lefever, Teo Macero, Judy M. Mathis, Robert McBride, A.E. McDonell, Jack McKenzie, Ramon Meyer, Malloy Miller, James L. Moore, Bo Nilsson, Donovan Olson, Acton Ostling, Joseph Ott, Gen Parchman, Richard Paschke, Albert Payson, Gordon Peters, G. David Peters, Mitchell Peters, Ted Petersen, Daniel Pinkham, A.E. Planchart, Paul Price.

Other composers from that bibliography include Robert Prince, Emil Raah, John Rapp, Dale Rauschenberg, Gardner Read, Don Ross, Armand Russell, W. Russell, James Salmon, Harold Schiffman, William Schinstine, Arthur Schnabel, Dick Schory, Brent Seawell, Truman Shoaff, Netty Simons, Bill Sindelar, Thomas Siwe, Warren Smith, Lewis Songer, Gitta Steiner, Karlheinz Stockhausen, Gerald Strang, Carlos Surinach, Duanne Thamm, Joel Thome, Virgil Thompson, Bob Tubes, David A. Tobias, Edgard Varese, Edward W. Voltz, Val. S. Vore, Rudolph Wagner-Regeny, Norman Ward, Frank Ward, Cary T. Whitmer, J. Kent Williams, Charles Wuorinen.

This listing of 1968 published composers may seem somewhat exhaustive, of course. However, it gives one a realistic view of the music for percussionists that was available at that time.

Following is an abbreviated list of titles from the 1968 compilation. For the purpose of simplicity, quotation marks have been omitted. The pieces of music include Music for Eleven, Discussion, Gatatumba, A Stopwatch and an Ordinance Map, Music for String Instruments and Percussion and Celesta, Sonata for Two Pianos and Percussion, Concerto for Marimba and Orchestra, Polyphonies for Percussion, Symphony for Drums, Divertimento, Sextet, Music for a Farce, Serie, Setting for Voice and Percussion, Pattern Percussion, Suite, Dialogue for Solo Percussion and Piano, Amores, Ceremonial March for Brass and Percussion, Mudras, Rondo for Percussion and Brass Instruments, The Golden Bubble, Quartet, Soliloquy of a Bhikunsi, Yu Ko, Concertino for Timpani, Fanfare for the Common Man.

Other titles from 1968 include Declamation for Brass and Percussion, Toccatina, Fantasia, Progressions, Divertimento for Violoncello and Percussion, Concerto for Percussion, Cantata para America Magica, A Scary Time, Canticle No. 3, Etudes for Audiences, March for Timpani and Brass, The Flowering Peach, Celebration, Sonant, Dance Sonata, Intrada Festiva, Nonet for Brass and Percussion, Litany and Prayer, Geigy Festival Concerto, Adventures, Entrance and Exit Music, For Seven, Suite de Variations for Ondes Martenot and Piano and Percussion, Concerto for Percussion (Mayuzumi), Sphenogrammes, Pastorale, Song for Trombone and Percussion, Improvisation for Batterie and Piano, Concerto for Marimba and Vibraphone, Basho Songs for Soprano and Percussion, Paul Bunyan Jump, Dark Forest, Soliloquy and Scherzo, Quintetto Concertante, Fantasy, Concerto for Five Kettledrums, Lamentations and Praises.

Other titles of music compositions include Homunculus C.F., Fanfare and Aria and Echo, Concerto for Percussion and Full Orchestra, Music for Seven Players, Fantasy for Toy Drums and Piano, The Emperor of Ice Cream, Serenade for Clarinet and Percussion, Sonata for Percussion and Piano, Three Dance Movements, Septet, Concerto for Trumpet and Percussion and Wind Orchestra, Refrain, Introduction and Rondo, Ritmo Jondo, Music, Bridges I, Chamber Piece No. 1, Trios I and II and III, March and Polonaise, Say Now Ye Lovely Social Band, Concerto for Timpani and Orchestra, Four Pieces for Brass Quintet and Timpani, A Witness for My Lord, Epithalamium, Sinfonietta, Tone Poem, Festfanfare, Triptych, Three Fanfares. This encompasses chamber music for percussion and other instruments. There may be some small typing errors, since the word processor and even the typewriter with automatic correction was not plentiful in 1968.

The following list of titles incorporates percussion ensembles. These include Allegre Muchacho, Ashland High, Holiday Special, London Bridge, Tom-Tom Foolery, Percussion on the Prowl, Ballet Mechanique, Estudio, Cressida, Rhythmic, A Dance, Four Stories, Trio for Percussion, Spielstuck, Percussion Suite, Three Movements, Waltz, Two Poems for Jazz, Modulation, La Musica Notturna di Madrid, Kaleidoscope, Galaxy, Auriga, First Quartet, Ensembolero, Percussionata, Three by Three, Introduction and Fugue, Short Overture for Percussion, Cartridge Music, Double Music, First Construction in Metal, Counterpoint for Percussions, Triple Threat, Pentatonic Clock, Tambuco, Toccata for Percussion Instruments, Quotations in Percussion, Percussion Quintet, Ostinato Pianissimo, Flat Baroque, Two for Six, Waltz for Swingers, Quintet for

Mallet Percussion. More titles of percussion ensembles from 1968 are Variations on a Four Note Theme, Theme and Variations, Petite Xylo, Encore in Jazz, Beautiful Jersey Shores, Six Ceremonial Fanfares, Juxtaposition No. 1, Mosaic No. 1, Tabla Dance, Tabla Tahmeel No. 1, Rhythm and Colors, Fragments, Lament, Latin Ostinato, March Rondo, Retrograde Waltz, Three Plus Two, Spain, Tarantella, Three Studies in Fours, Chamber Sonata, The African Story, Canon for Percussion, Scherzo for Percussion, Parade for Percussion Ensemble, Two Marches, Percussive Panorama, Drummers Five, Five Up Front, Colonel Irons, The Elmhurst Quintet, Rataplan, Fifth Symphony, Fugue, The Song of Queztecoatl, Liaisons, Air Express, Academic Ensembles, October Mountain. The range of creativity among percussion composers is, without doubt, practically endless. Here are more titles of percussion ensembles from 1968: Toy Concerto, Marginal Sounds, Durango, Monticello, Shiprock, Adventure, First Structure, Jingle Jangle, Invasion, Nonet, Introduction and Allegro, Dolidrums, Sketches in Sound, Toccata without Instruments, Les Petits Symphonistes, Tympanorum Musices, Eighteen Heads, Banana Boat Calypso, Characters Three, Interiors, Reaktionen, Drummer's Patrol, Procession of the Gnomes, Ricercare for Percussion, Symphony for Percussion Ensemble, The Swords of Moda-Ling, Neumes Triebend, A La Naningo, March of the Eagles, Percussion Piece, Easter Cantata, Divertimento for Percussion Trio, Batter Up--Snare Down, The Epic of Western Man, Sounds of the City.

More titles, many of which the experienced percussion instructor will recognize, include Skirmish, Los Dioses Aztecas, Ritimica V, Percussion Studies in Cuban Rhythm, Musica Battuta, Keystone Kids, Overlap, Rhythm Busters, Suspense and the Walking Man, Woodland Drive, Duodecimet, Bapa, The Frustrated Percussionist, Scope, Destination Five, Design Groups for Percussion, Showcase, Duet for Timpani and Snare Drum, Introduction and Samba, Crab-Canon for Three Percussion, Night Music for Percussion, Zyklus, Le Cirque, Hollywood Carnival, Bellwood Six, Rolling Progress, Sonic Boom, Drums on the 'Phone, Fanfare for France, Blue Percussion, Concert Asiatique, Ionization, Prelude and Allegro for Percussion Ensemble, Impact, African Sketches, Prelude and Fugue.

In conclusion, this survey of music from the 1960s presents a vital, beautiful look at rather recent history. One should keep in mind that sometimes composers select a piece's title, and sometimes the publisher chooses. This list, however, gives a good scan of some of the pedagogy in percussion that was popular three decades ago. At that time, percussion was just earning its place in concert music, based upon developments of the past few centuries. Ethnic music, classical, romantic and jazz were able to be performed well with percussion instruments in formal settings.

Composer's Notes

The art and craft of music composition is a relatively new field in the history of the human species. In the western world, specifically Europe, music notation was developed during the Middle Ages or Medieval period of music history. This period can be said to have originated about the Fourth Century A.D. and closed with the beginning of the Renaissance at about the middle of the 15th Century.

By the time of composers Machaut, Isaac, Byrd, Monteverdi and Bach, music notation was quite well developed. This was a development of more than a thousand years, however, for there are extant a few music examples from the historical period preceding the Middle Ages, Antiquity.

Music notation in the 20th Century has been in a consistent state of development, too. Graphic notation, aleatoric music, improvisation notation and electronic music all offer the composer a few challenges in regard to writing it down.

This author has written more than a hundred music compositions since the middle of the century, with a specialty in percussion. Problems of notation, especially, have been addressed in this project.

The music of Bach and Mozart have served as good models for this author, and much has been learned from contemporaries such as Beck, Crumb, Carter, Stockhausen, Haubenstock-Ramati, Brown and Becker, to name only a few. Following is an alphabetized list of original titles, accompanied by notations.

Larrick, Geary. A 16th Century Poem. Stevens Point, Wisconsin: G and L Publishing, 1993. This duo for voice and marimba is in art song style. It was reviewed in a percussion journal published in France.

Larrick, Geary. A Musical Joke. Stevens Point: G and L, 1985. Composed in Seremban, Malaysia, this Composition for A Car can be performed by one to three players. The sounds are percussive in nature.

Larrick, Geary. A Repertory List. Stevens Point: G and L, 1992. This duo for percussion and reader, includes directions for the improvising percussionist. It

51

was presented in Stevens Point at two preschool classes, at the university in the Collins Classroom Center, and on Community Access Television. Instrument selection varied.

Larrick, Geary. A Song of Moses. Stevens Point: G and L, 1993. Printed in typescript, the text is from the King James edition of the Bible. Percussion instrumentation includes snare drum, marimba, tom-toms and cymbals. The text is read. Dedicated to Nexus.

Larrick, Geary. Adagio for Marimba. Stevens Point: G and L, 1987. Dedicated to C.H. Fang, this solo was originally written for violin. The author performed it on xylophone in Pittsburgh, Pennsylvania, in November, 1997, at the Byham Theatre, for a group representing the newly founded Malaysian Philharmonic Orchestra. Deagan mallets were used with a Deagan instrument having rosewood keys.

Larrick, Geary. Adagio with Accompaniment. Stevens Point: G and L, 1989. This one-page typed score is for violin and hand drum. It was performed by the author at Gesell Institute in Wisconsin.

Larrick, Geary. Ballad for Angklung Choir and Organ. Stevens Point: G and L, 1987. Several bamboo angklungs are required for this piece. It was conducted by the author at St. Paul's United Methodist Church in Stevens Point, Wisconsin.

Larrick, Geary. Ballad for JB. Stevens Point: G and L, 1988. This lead sheet can be read by a keyboard percussionist playing marimba or vibraphone. It is entitled for the director of the Portage County Health and Human Services department, Judy Bablitch. It has been performed by the author in Michelsen Hall in the Fine Arts Center at the University of Wisconsin at Stevens Point on piano, and performed in a combo on drum set by John H. Beck in Rochester, New York. The author has played the piece many times on piano and marimba, in addition to a presentation on vibes on Saturday, May 6, 2000, for the grand opening of the new addition at the Stevens Point Area YMCA.

Larrick, Geary. Ballad for Joey. Stevens Point: G and L, 1988. This four-mallet vibe solo is six pages in length, including the cover and title page. MusIc typography was done by Donald Jones in Rochester, New York.

Larrick, Geary. Ballad for Joey, Arranged for Marimba. Stevens Point: G and L, 1989. This version for solo marimba is typed on four pages. It is entitled for Joey Fang, a graduate of the University of Wisconsin at Stevens Point and the University of Miami in Florida.

Larrick, Geary. Blues for JG. Stevens Point: G and L, 1999. This solo for vibraphone is entitled for John Galm, Boulder, Colorado. The piece is two pages in hand manuscript.

Larrick, Geary. Boston for Violin and Marimba. Stevens Point: G and L, 1989. This duo was written by adapting a previously composed piece titled "February for violin. The marimba part is notated on the grand staff, with both treble and bass clefs.

Larrick, Geary. Cadenza. Stevens Point: G and L, 1988. This one-page typed solo for marimba or xylophone, was composed in 1967 in Cambridge, Ohio. Its theme is based upon the well known "Hora Staccato" by Dinicu and Heifetz. The author has performed it at Muskingum College, at the University of Colorado on July 4, at the University of Arkansas, at Amherst High School and with the wind ensemble for the University of Wisconsin at Stevens Point.

Larrick, Geary. Chamber Symphony. Stevens Point: G and L, 1990. This First Symphony, for percussion, has a forty-five page typed score. Instrumentation includes piano, celesta, chimes, orchestra bells, vibraphone, xylophone, marimba, temple blocks, cowbells, brake drums, bass drum, snare drum, slapstick, tom-tom, suspended cymbal, guiro, castanets, maracas, wind chimes, tambourine and triangle. The four movements are subtitled "Fanfare and March," "Meditation," "Waltz" and "Galop.

Larrick, Geary. Chorale with Variations. Stevens Point: G and L, 1988. This work for four marimbas was started on the south side of Cambridge, Ohio, in 1978. It was conducted by the author in the Fine Arts Center at the University of Wisconsin at Stevens Point.

Larrick, Geary. Composition for Snare Drum. Stevens Point: G and L, 1985. This three movement sonatina was developed with the assistance of Chicago Symphony Orchestra snare drummer A. Payson. This particular publication includes a page of performance notes.

Larrick, Geary. Composition No. 2. Stevens Point: G and L, 1985. This three movement piece for snare drum was composed in Kuala Lumpur, Malaysia. The second movement, subtitled "The Five Oranges," was inspired by a dish of fruit on the kitchen table of the residence where it was composed.

Larrick, Geary. Composition No. 3. Stevens Point: G and L, 1989. This solo for snare drum is eleven pages in typescript. The three movements are subtitled "Sonata Form," "Rondo" and "Minuet."

Larrick, Geary. Composition No. 11. Stevens Point: G and L, 2000. This short three movement solo for drum is subtitled "Morning," "Noon" and "Afternoon." Meters are four-four, three-four and five-four. It is in hand manuscript.

Larrick, Geary. Duo for Alto Saxophone and Snare Drum. Stevens Point: G and L, 1993. This twelve-page typed score was inspired by the chair of the Department of Music in the College of Fine Arts and Communication at the University of Wisconsin at Stevens Point, a saxophonist who graduated from Northwestern University in Evanston, Illinois.

Larrick, Geary. Duo for Contrabass and Percussion. Stevens Point: G and L, 1991. This duet for double bass and multipercussion, utilizes three suspended cymbals indicated low, medium and high in sound. Various types of sticks and mallets are requested for use.

Larrick, Geary. Duo for Crotales and Harpsichord. Stevens Point: G and L, 1997. Duration of this piece is more than three minutes, requesting tuned antique cymbals. It was written at the suggestion of a music professor at the University of Iowa.

Larrick, Geary. Duo for Percussion. Stevens Point: G and L, 1991. This set of typed score and parts includes an acknowledgment and setup directions. Instrumentation is marimba, timpani, slapstick and temple blocks. It was written at the motivation of a professional duo in Europe.

Larrick, Geary. Duo Sonata. Stevens Point: G and L, 1985. This piece for trombone and multipercussion is for snare drum, suspended cymbal, brake drums and temple blocks. It received a New York City performance, and the author has performed it in Colorado and Wisconsin. The duet was composed in Rochester, New York, during summer of 1980, for a class with Samuel Adler.

Larrick, Geary. Ecclesiasticus. Stevens Point: G and L, 1989. This three-page typed solo for marimba is sacred, or classical, in style. It calls for a four-and-a-third octave instrument, but of course can be played effectively on smaller ones. The author has presented in liturgy at Saint Paul's United Methodist Church in central Wisconsin.

Larrick, Geary. <u>Elegie</u>. Stevens Point: G and L, 1988. This one-page typed score for solo marimba is notated on the grand staff. It needs four mallets in a true interpretation.

Larrick, Geary. <u>Elegy and Meditation</u>. Stevens Point: G and L, 1987. This solo for marimba was played by the author for a meeting of the Wisconsin chapter of the Percussive Arts Society near Madison, hosted by J. Latimer.

Larrick, Geary. <u>Etude for JB</u>. Stevens Point: G and L, 1998. This solo for percussion requires three sets of wind chimes. It is entitled for John H. Beck. The author performed the piece on a program in Michelsen Hall on a program of American music sponsored by a chapter of Phi Mu Alpha Sinfonia.

Larrick, Geary. <u>Fanfare</u>. Stevens Point: G and L, 1987. This brief work for symphony orchestra was composed while the author was timpanist of the Central Wisconsin Symphony Orchestra. It requests a rather large percussion section including timpani, marimba and xylophone. The idea of the last timpani note played without roll is borrowed from music of Tchaikovsky.

Larrick, Geary. <u>Four Pieces for Clarinet and Sounds</u>. Stevens Point: G and L, 1989. The "sounds" include suspended cymbal played with brushes, and vibraphone. The author performed this work, originally composed in 1975, in Michelsen Hall in the Fine Arts Center at the University of Wisconsin at Stevens Point. The music, in typescript, has been performed in Europe.

Larrick, Geary. <u>Happy New Millennium</u>. Stevens Point: G and L, 1999. This piece for solo marimba was composed on December 9, 1999, in Stevens Point. It is in a classical style based upon Latin American music.

Larrick, Geary. <u>Improvisation for Drum</u>. Stevens Point: G and L, 1999. This one-page set of directions includes rhythmic motives for each of three movements. The drum performer could then play a set of variations similar in form to those played by drum set players when "taking a break" in a jazz presentation.

Larrick, Geary. <u>Improvisational Suite</u>. Stevens Point: G and L, 1992. This set of directions, for solo percussion, describes the author's premiere presentation. It suggests movement subtitles in regard to the four seasons. The author found this work to be especially successful in youth concert situations, with an emphasis on a multicultural collection of instruments.

Larrick, Geary. <u>Lyric Piece</u>. Stevens Point: G and L, 1985. This duo for alto recorder and metallophone can be played with flute and bells, though the

55

percussion definite pitches may sound atonal. It was inspired by the author's excellent experiences playing the alto recorder in the 1960s and 1970s, first in a trio with harpsichord and violoncello, then later with harpsichord accompaniment. A metallophone was constructed with interesting results.

Larrick, Geary. Marie. Columbus, Ohio: Permus Publications, 1978. This four-mallet rag for marimba or vibes, was composed in the Department of Music in the Fine Arts Center at the University of Wisconsin in Stevens Point in spring, 1975. The author also plays it with two mallets. The piece has enjoyed widespread distribution including Europe and the U.S.

Larrick, Geary. Melody for Abraham Lincoln. Stevens Point: G and L Publishing, 1989. This duet for oboe and multipercussion utilizes a vibraphone, cymbal and drum. The six-page score is in typescript. The piece represents the new 20th Century definition of "melody," as demonstrated in the field of percussion.

Larrick, Geary. Melody in F. Stevens Point: G and L, 2000. This solo for marimba is thirty-six measures in length, in hand manuscript. Time signature is five-four, indicated lively. The melody was worked out by the author in August, 1972, while driving solo from Colorado to Wisconsin following doctoral study.

Larrick, Geary. Missa Brevis. Stevens Point: G and L, 1993. This typed score for percussion ensemble has five movements subtitled "Kyrie," "Gloria," "Credo," "Sanctus-Benedictus" and "Agnus Dei." Instrumentation is marimba, bells, xylophone, drums and cymbals. It is a 20th Century version of a Medieval musical mass similar to that written by Machaut and following composers. Other influences came from the pen of Bach, Beethoven and Berlioz. Like an elegy, its primary function is to elicit beauty from music.

Larrick, Geary. Ode To A Menominee. Stevens Point: G and L, 1985. This quintet for percussion and flute includes marimba, vibraphone, maracas, tom-toms and snare drums. It was conducted by the author with the University Percussion Ensemble at a concert in Michelsen Hall in the Fine Arts Center at the University of Wisconsin-Stevens Point, with good audience response. Preparation for the writing was done with research in libraries of Stevens Point, including listening to recordings of music by Native Americans. It was inspired by hearing a man named Moon speak in public.

Larrick, Geary. Piece for Flute and Drums. Stevens Point: G and L, 1985. This duo for flute and tom-toms begins Andante moving toward Vivace. Its typescript is on three pages. The historic fife and drum combination was an inspiration for the composition of this work, the first of a series.

Larrick, Geary. Piece No. 2. Stevens Point: G and L, 1989. This duo for flute and percussion calls for four drums played with the hands. Of course, drum sticks may be used in good taste.

Larrick, Geary. Piece No. 3. Stevens Point: G and L, 1992. This chamber music for flutes and wind chimes is two and a half minutes in duration. Of course it may be repeated any number of times. The combination should sound well.

Larrick, Geary. Piece No. 5. Stevens Point: G and L, 1998. This duo for flute and drum sounds best if played on piccolo flute and piccolo drum. A piccolo drum measures approximately three or four inches deep and fourteen inches across the diameter of the batter, or top, head. It was composed after the author played on a piccolo snare drum in Sentry Theater with the Central Wisconsin Symphony Orchestra.

Larrick, Geary. Poem with Accompaniment. Stevens Point: G and L, 1990. This duo for viola and timpani was adapted from the author's earlier "Poem for the Viola," which was also published in a literary magazine produced by the University of Wisconsin at Stevens Point. The drums may be played with brushes or mallets, depending upon circumstances. Prevention of damage to the timpani heads would be important, while achievement of a good, effective sound is primary.

Larrick, Geary. Quintet for Drumline. Stevens Point: G and L, 1985. This neo-Baroque music calls for four drums and a cymbal player. It was composed in Ohio, Guernsey and Muskingum counties. The piece is in typescript, score and parts, and was conducted by the author in Michelsen Hall in central Wisconsin.

Larrick, Geary. Quintet for Trumpets and Timpani. Stevens Point: G and L, 1991. The trumpet quartet was inspired while listening one Sunday morning at St. Paul's United Methodist Church in Stevens Point, to a group led by J. Adams. The four timpani can be played by one performer.

Larrick, Geary. Rag. Stevens Point: G and L, 1989. This marimba solo is based on ideas learned from a retired vaudeville performer, Al "Rags" Anderson, with whom the author studied in Columbus, Ohio, during middle chool. In 2000, the author has been playing the work in the key of B-flat, rather than in the notated key of F major.

Larrick, Geary. <u>Repertory List II</u>. Plover, Wisconsin: G and L Publishing, 1998. This improvised duo was performed by the author on tambourine with tape recorder for a conference at the University Center in Stevens Point. The reader part was then pre-recorded on audio cassette tape.

Larrick, Geary. <u>Scott's Tune</u>. Holcomb, New York: William L. Cahn Publishing, 1985. Entitled for the author's son, Scott, this marimba solo in ragtime style can be played with four or fewer mallets. It also works on vibraphone.

Larrick, Geary. <u>Seven Easy Pieces for Drum</u>. Stevens Point, Wisconsin: G and L Publishing, 1995.

This solo study in dynamics was composed in Malaysia. It was performed for Community Access Television in Stevens Point. The descriptive term "easy" is at times questionable.

Larrick, Geary. <u>Six Drum Cadences</u>. Stevens Point: G and L, 1995. For the most part, these cadences originated in the 1960s in Cambridge, Ohio, when the author was teaching public school. They were then notated in Singapore in 1995, while the author was visiting the home of. two graduates of the University of Wisconsin at Stevens Point. One of the "six," titled "The Woodchuck," was composed in early evening in Seremban, Malaysia.

Larrick, Geary. <u>Sketch for Marimba</u>. Stevens Point: G and L, 1998. This solo for three or four mallets is in hand manuscript on the grand staff. It is based upon a study of the music of F. Chopin.

Larrick, Geary. <u>Sonata for Bass Drum</u>. Stevens Point: G and L, 1985. This First Sonata for solo percussion was performed by John Beck in Bydgoszcz, Poland, for an international percussion workshop. The author composed it in 1974 in Aspen, Colorado. Other composers in Aspen that summer were Brown, Carter and Crumb. Typescript is by Donald Jones. The piece has been performed in Idaho and Ohio, and by the author several places around Wisconsin.

Larrick, Geary. <u>Sonata No. 7</u>. Stevens Point: G and L, 1991. This solo for timpani is dedicated to J.H. Beck, Rochester, New York. Movement subtitles are "Majestic," "Slow," "Bright" and "Fast." Its main concept is one of tone production with musical beauty.

Larrick, Geary. <u>Sonata No. 8</u>. Stevens Point: G and L, 1991. This solo for marimba is dedicated to J.L. Moore in central Ohio. Movement subtitles are "Raindrops," "Wind," "Sunshine" and "Snow." It was recorded by the author on video tape in the studio of Community Access Television in Stevens Point. Its primary concept is pointillism with steady rhythm and tonal melody.

Larrick, Geary. Stars and Stripes II. Stevens Point: G and L, 1998. This three minute solo for marimba utilizes the grand staff. Recommended tempo for this classical piece is one hundred eighteen counts per minute, like a Sousa march.

Larrick, Geary. Symphony for Band. Stevens Point: G and L, 1992. This thirty-five page typed score is appropriate also for wind ensemble, wind orchestra and wind symphony. The four movements are subtitled 'Adagio," "Allegro," "Scherzo" and "Finale." The three percussion parts include snare drum, triangle, suspended cymbal, xylophone, clash cymbals, wood block, tom-tom, bass drum, chimes and orchestra bells. The author conducted a read through several years ago with The Crenadiers Band in Stevens Point at Lincoln Senior Center.

Larrick, Geary. Symphony No. 3. Stevens Point; G and L, 1993. This thirty-nine page typed score is for string orchestra, oboes and timpani. It is perhaps neo-Baroque in style.

Larrick, Geary. Symphony No. 4. Stevens Point: G and L, 1993. This forty page typed score is written for woodwind choir and percussion. The three percussion parts utilize marimba, snare drum, tambourine, triangle and wood block.

Larrick, Geary. The Story of Punkin Person. Stevens Point: G and L, 1989. This suite for narrator, brass quintet and percussion can utilize the standard drum set. It was conducted by the author in Michelsen Hall in the Fine Arts Center at the University of Wisconsin at Stevens Point for a Composers Forum program directed by Dr. Leon Smith. Its concept is based upon experiences the author had as a public school orchestra director, leading youth concerts in elementary schools. The music ranges from atonality to ragtime, with a circus ending.

Larrick, Geary. The Temple Garden. Stevens Point: G and L, 1989. This eight page score is for glockenspiel and piano. Movement subtitles are "Dawn," "Mid-morning," "Early Afternoon," "Late Afternoon" and "Dusk." It is dedicated to Milwaukee percussionist Tele Lesbines.

Larrick, Geary. The Three Daughters. Stevens Point: G and L, 1988. Style of this percussion quintet is ragtime. Instrumentation is xylophone, three marimbas and multipercussion. It is dedicated to Nexus percussion ensemble of

Toronto. Inspiration for its composition came as a result of a successful birth of the author's only daughter in a moment of glory, following two failures.

Larrick, Geary. Trio for Handclappers. Stevens Point: C and L, 1990. This spright trio was performed in Philadelphia, Pennsylvania, at an Eastman Alumni Concert directed by a graduate of the University of Rochester. The author performed it at the College of Professional Studies building in Stevens Point, for a youth group taught by Lorrie Richardson. Other performers for that presentation at Gesell Institute were a student and drum set artist S. Zenz. The piece was inspired by hand clapping compositions that the author conducted previously by composer Warren Benson and others. This trio is in typescript, with score and parts.

Larrick, Geary. Trio for Tambourines. Stevens Point: G and L, 1990. This light percussion ensemble was presented by the author at Gesell Institute with percussionist Steve Zenz and.a student, for a class taught by L. Richardson. The publication set includes typed score and parts. A concert approach to playing the tambourine is recommended for this piece, rather than popular style. It is a good demonstration piece for young audiences, since many general music classrooms contain tambourines. Also, later in life, musicians often play the tambourine in rock music groups and lounge acts.

Larrick, Ceary. Trio Sonata. Stevens Point: C and L, 1988. This monumental work is dedicated to The Percussion Group - Cincinnati. It calls for three timpanists with four drums each, and was favorably reviewed in publication by a professor in Texas for the Percussive Arts Society. The idea was conceived based upon the author's experience playing four of twelve timpani playing a tone row in music of Penderecki with the Eastman Wind Ensemble in the Eastman Theatre in Rochester, New York, under the baton of Dr. Donald Hunsberger. This concert was recorded and later released by Deutsche Grammophon. The publication is printed with parts only, although the conductor of a group could draw up a score if needed. It is probably more tonal than dodecaphonic.

Larrick, Geary. Twojazz. Stevens Point: G and L, 1988. This duo for trumpet and vibraphone was practice tested by the author and trumpetist Joseph Adams. The B-flat trumpet part has a key signature of three sharps. The music is in a lilting, relaxed style.

Larrick, Geary. Vivo Duo. Stevens Point: G and L, 1988. This duet for trumpet and vibraharp, four mallets, is written without key signature. It is in typescript, and in score printed format.

Larrick, Geary. Waiting and Accompaniment. Stevens Point: G and L, 1990. This duo for marimba and cello is based upon the author's solo "Waiting" that was composed while the author was waiting for a colleague, Charles Goan, to arrive one day for lunch. C. Goan was the author's piano accompanist in my first Wisconsin recital in spring, 1970, in Main Auditorium in Stevens Point for a performance of Peter Tanner's "Sonata for Marimba." The auditorium was full of listeners that evening, for a program that included a new piece by faculty member Dean Blair, vibraphone music by S. De Castyne, timpani music by J. Bergamo, and "The Soldier's Tale" by Igor Stravinsky, conducted by Dr. Robert Van Nuys. Music historian E. McLott wrote the program notes. Some of the recital was a repeat of works played by the author a year preceding in Kilbourn Hall at Eastman. The marimba part to "Waiting and Accompaniment" starts on the grand staff.

In conclusion, the preceding bibliography with notes, is an example of what can be produced by a small business in a small city in the upper midwest from 1985 to 2000. This essay includes only those with percussion. Assistance was derived from The Small Business Development Center at the University of Wisconsin at Stevens Point, with an office in Old Main.

Compositions Reference

Music in Print Master Composer Index 1999. Philadelphia, Pennsylvania: Musicdata, 1999. Volume XCa, page 580.

Larrick, Geary. Adagio with Accompaniment. Boston. Duo for Double Bass and Percussion. Poem with Accompaniment. Waiting and Accompaniment.

These five compositions by the author are among twelve listed in the 1999 Master Composer Index. They are duos with percussion and a stringed instrument. Original publication was by G and L Publishing of Stevens Point, Wisconsin, founded by the author in 1985.

As a performer, the author has played the "Adagio with Accompaniment" at Gesell Institute at the University of Wisconsin-Stevens Point. Collaborators included a violinist from the Central Wisconsin Symphony Orchestra, and teachers J. Gingles, J. Malone and L. Richardson. The audience consisted of young children and parents, including the author's daughter. It was well received.

Contemporary Topics

Since this is essentially a history book, it may be relevant to take a look at areas that surround the percussionist in society at the beginning of the 21st Century. Indeed, the 20th Century saw many changes in regard to technology and information. Among these changes was music for percussion that, likewise, changed from decade to decade.

At the beginning of the 20th Century, Stravinsky was writing music that incorporated percussion in new ways, compared with the past. Examples are "The Rite of Spring" and "The Soldier's Tale." At about 1930, the percussion ensemble came into being, with music composed by Cage and Varese. At mid-century, Carter was writing solo timpani pieces, then Stockhausen composed a multipercussion solo, *"Zyklus,"* that calls for twenty instruments played by one person.

In the second half of the century, world music became important, with western percussionists going to Africa, South America and elsewhere to study the local musics. These ideas were then transferred to a new music. For example, Asian and American ideas have been used successfully in the development of what can be called multicultural music. This is in cultural agreement with many people of the world, who have a multicultural ancestral heritage.

Also, the borrowing of ideas from the past, such as the sonata type, has produced a contemporary composition beside those that utilize new technology such as the computer and the synthesizer. Following is a rather broad collection of sources that reflect contemporary society, affecting the percussion music that is produced, composed, performed and improvised.

"About this Issue." Computer Music Journal 21/2 (Summer 1997), 1.

Bailey, Benjamin. "Communication of Respect in Interethnic Service Encounters." Language in Society 26/3 (September 1997), 327.

Behague, Gerard. Music in Latin America: An Introduction. Englewood Cliffs, New Jersey: Prentice-Hall, 1979.

Drass, Kriss A. and Cregware, Peter R. and Musheno, Michael. "Social, Cultural and Temporal Dynamics of the AIDS Case Congregation: Early Years of the Epidemic." Law and Society Review 31/2 (1997), 267.

Galambos, DSW, Colleen M. "Quality of Life for the Elder: A Reality or an Illusion?" Journal of Gerontological Social Work 27/3 (1997), 27.

Grim, John A. "Cultural Identity, Authenticity and Community Survival: The Politics of Recognition in the Study of Native American Religions." American Indian Quarterly 20/3 (Summer 1996), 353.

Huang, Hao. "Music Appreciation Class: Broadening Perspectives." Music Educators Journal 84/2 (September 1997), 29.

Larrick, Geary. "A Drummer's View of 1984." Faculty Forum 1/3 (April 1979), 3.

Larrick, Ceary. "Proper Angklung Technique." Percussive Notes 28/3 (Spring 1990), 59.

Larrick, Geary. "Science and Percussion Music." Wisconsin Percussive Arts Society Newsletter 19/1 (January 1991), 2.

Larrick, Geary. "The Creative Youth Concert." Brass and Percussion 11/4 (Fall 1974), 12.

Malm, William P. Music Cultures of the Pacific, the Near East and Asia. Englewood Cliffs: PrenticeHall, 1977.

Shaffer, Frank. "Practicing with Mind and Body As You Recover From an Injury." Percussive Notes 38/3 (June 2000), 65.

Cymbal History

Following is a personal history of the author's experience with the percussion instrument called cymbals. It is ordered chronologically, with some dates approximate.

1963 - Cymbals, position L-1, Ohio State University Marching Band, J. Evans, director. I had one week to learn the technique before the first public performance. The technique included gripping the leather straps so that the cymbals could be twirled in a rhythmic sequence. Part of the job was to clean and polish the cymbals regularly.

1964 - Cymbals on music of Sousa featured in the center of the American Wind Symphony Orchestra in Pittsburgh and on tour in summer, including the twirling technique. Another piece on which the author performed the cymbals with this organization featured a male singer in an arrangement of Ol' Man River. This was appropriate, since the ensemble performed on a barge with an acoustic shell for concerts on American waterways such as the Ohio and Mississippi Rivers. Concerts were given in Pittsburgh, Morgantown, Paducah, Saint Louis and elsewhere. In autumn, the author again played cymbals for the OSU Marching Band, using a pair of concert cymbals in Mershon Auditorium for recording the album Saturday Afternoon at Columbus, directed by C. Spohn.

1965 - As a member of the Baltimore Symphony Orchestra, the author used a suspended cymbal in music of Rimsky-Korsakov, in youth concerts played at the Lyric Theatre and in schools in the area and on tour including Saranac Lake, New York. Also, the author played bass drum on the Overture to Rossini's Barber of Seville. For the subscription concert series, the author played cymbals on a Wagner overture.

1966 - Teaching in summer at Foster Music Camp in Richmond, Kentucky, on the campus of Eastern Kentucky University, the author played cymbals in the orchestra on Carmen Suite arranged from opera music of Bizet. Also, cymbal instruction was given with work for the Cambridge, Ohio, High School Marching Band directed by R. Eubanks, and also the next school year for director M. Treier. The U.S. Marine Band presented a tour concert in Cambridge, and the author enjoyed the cymbal playing.

1968 - Cymbal lesson with John H. Beck at the Eastman School of Music of the University of Rochester in New York. The author played cymbals with the Eastman Wind Ensemble, and as principal percussionist in the Eastman Philharmonia.

1969 - The author played cymbals with the Rochester Philharmonic Orchestra in the Eastman Theatre and in Kilbourn Hall for conductors Hanson, Hendl and Page. Cymbals were also played in the Eastman Percussion Ensemble directed by J. Beck. Another performance was cymbals on Beethoven's Ninth Symphony at the Eastman School. Beginning later in the year, the author offered cymbal instruction in the Department of Music at Wisconsin State University, Stevens Point. This faculty position lasted until 1985 in active status.

1972 - From 1971 to 1973, and in 1975, the author played cymbals in the summer band in the College of Music at the University of Colorado, Boulder, for directors F. Baird and H. McMillen.

1974 - The author enjoyed a cymbal lesson with Charles Owen in Aspen, Colorado, where he was performing with the Festival Orchestra. The author was also able to hear the cymbals played in concert.

1980 - The author attended a concert at Symphony Hall in Chicago, Illinois, watching and listening to Chicago Symphony Orchestra percussionists Denov and Peters on cymbals. In summer, the author attended a Toronto Symphony performance at the auditorium at Ontario Place, enjoying watching and listening to the cymbal player, D. Ruddick, perform on Tchaikovsky's Fourth Symphony. Previously, in summer of 1968, the author played triangle on Tchaikovsky's Fourth with the Rochester Philharmonic at Highland Park, watching percussionist B. Becker play cymbals at the time.

1981 - The author performed antique cymbal on music of Debussy with percussionist D. Kaster in Sentry Theater in Stevens Point with the Central Wisconsin Symphony Orchestra, conducted by J. Borowicz.

1982 - The author played two small cymbals connected with a rope in the Collegium Musicum at the University of Colorado in recital. Attendance at Denver Symphony Orchestra concerts was a good source for learning, also.

1984 - The author played cymbals on Tchaikovsky's Fourth with the Central Wisconsin Symphony Orchestra. Earlier, in 1980 while attending summer school in Rochester, the author composed a Duo Sonata that utilizes suspended cymbals in the multipercussion part. The author performed this piece in Boulder, Stevens Point, and Milwaukee. Other performances have been in Missouri and New York City.

1986 - The author performed J.L. Moore's "Psalm Collage" with suspended cymbal for an early evening Christmas presentation in the sanctuary of St. Paul's United Methodist Church in Stevens Point, W. Carlson, pastor.

1987 - The author played cymbals on the National Anthem with the Stevens Point City Band at Pfiffner Park. This patriotic music was a part of the pre-game ceremony at OSU, when the author played in the Marching Band.

1988 - A Museum Gallery show titled The World of Percussion was presented by the author, E. Marks, curator, in the Learning Resources Center at the University of Wisconsin-Stevens Point, for a month. Background music for this show was the recording Nexus Now, including Bob Becker's "Cymbal." Later, the author heard this composition in performance by Nexus at a Percussive Arts Society International Convention.

1990 - The author's second book was published in Lewiston, New York, entitled Musical References and Song Texts in the Bible. It contains a section on cymbals with fifteen items.

1997 - The author composed "Duo for Crotales and Harpsichord" in Stevens Point, Wisconsin, for G and L Publishing. Crotales are tuned antique cymbals, mounted on a board and struck with mallets.

1990s - The author played suspended cymbal with the Grenadiers Band in Stevens Point at Lincoln Senior Center, in Plainfield at Thresherman's Park, at the Rosholt Lions Camp, and at the Rosholt Community Fair in the bandstand. Video recordings of the Ohio State University Marching Band, including the author playing cymbals, were released from the 1963 and 1964 seasons by Rare Sportsfilms in Naperville, Illinois, published by D. Ewing. Additionally, the author has composed music that includes cymbals in several instances.

Drum Duets

Lepak, Alexander. 26 Contemporary Snare Drum Duets. Windsor, Connecticut: Windsor Music Publications, 1991. This fifty-five page book cost $15.00 at the time of its publication. It is a softcover method book, dedicated to Arthur Perretta. Lepak specializes in writing for percussion instruments. Located in New England, Professor Lepak has taught percussionists that are nationally known, such as Tele Lesbines in the Milwaukee Symphony Orchestra on timpani and for a while principal percussion, and Emil Richards who is known for recording in the Los Angeles area.

Alexander Lepak is exemplary of an active generation of professional percussionists who practice in the areas of music business, performance and teaching. Other titles that he has produced include "Concerto for Mallet Instruments," "Control of the Drum Set--Phrasing for the Soloist," "Crescendo" for percussion enesmble, "Decrescendo" for percussion and brass, "Duo" for timpani, "Fifty Contemporary Snare Drum Etudes," "Suite for Solo Vibraphone," and "Thirty-two Solos" for timpani.

In the publisher's Percussion Ensemble Jazz Series, Mr. Lepak has produced original compositions as well as arrangements. These authoritative publications are written for the college student, and would be appropriate for reading by the talented secondary school student.

The Drum Duet book contains music with an emphasis upon rhythm. Performance notes point out elements of detail, technique and interpretation.

Notation in this book is clear and easy to read. The notes of varying values are typed on a usual five line staff, with occasional changing meters. For example, Duet 8 begins in 5/8 meter, with changes to 3/4, 5/8 and so forth, alternating throughout the piece. Duet 16 is notated without bar lines, while Duet #17 suggests contrasting sounds. Metronome indications for specific tempo suggestions are given at the beginning of each etude. Accents, dynamics, rhythm and rolls are accentuated.

These could be played on practice pads, or on two drums of different sizes. Likewise, the player could vary the snare type like nylon, wire or gut. Sizes of drums could range from piccolo, about 3" x 14" to dance drum, 5" x 14" to concert drum, 6 1/2" x 14" to marching drum, 10" x 14". These are not exclusive, of course.

71

The Drum Set

Black, Dave. Drumset Independence and Syncopation. Van Nuys, California: Alfred Publishing, 1998.

Feldstein, Sandy and Black, Dave. Alfred's Beginning Drumset Method. Van Nuys: Alred Publishing, 1990.

Fullen, Brian and Vogt, Roy. Contemporary Country Styles. Van Nuys: Alfred Publishing, 1994.

Larrick, Geary and Kawleski, Terrance. "Drumming Can Be A Listener's Art." NACWPI Journal XXX/2 (Winter 1982), 8.

Wheeler, Douglas. "Music Reviews." Review of In the Pocket for four drum sets, composed by John Beck, published in 1999 by Kendor Music. NACWPI Journal XLVIII/4 (Summer 2000), 14.

The basic drum set has been a popular music instrument in the 20th Century. It consists of a snare drum on a stand, bass drum on the floor with attached foot pedal beater, two tom-toms that are fastened above the bass drum, a ride cymbal suspended on a stand, perhaps a crash cymbal, and two high-hat cymbals played with a foot pedal. Seated on a drum throne, the percussionist or drummer can thus perform in a multipercussion setup.

The number of cymbals can he added, as can the number of tom-toms. In a Broadway musical situation, the player may also use a small xylophone, timpani, wood block, triangle and chimes typically.

The drum set is used often in jazz, rock and country musics, and in symphony orchestras for pops concerts. Double bass drums are sometimes included for special effects. Jazz groups that incorporate the drum set include combos and big bands.

In the early part of the 20th Century, the bass drum foot pedal beater was an important invention. One of the well known inventors was William Ludwig, Sr., who founded the Ludwig Drum Company in Chicago. Darius Milhaud called for the foot pedal bass drum with attached cymbal striker in his "Concerto for Percussion" and small orchestra. This author was pleased to perform the Concerto with wind band in Colorado and with two pianos accompanying in Wisconsin. The cymbal striker was able to be manipulated by the player so that it could be silent as well. Indeed, the sound of bass drum and cymbal struck together is impressive and effective for certain passages of music. The drum set player often uses the pedal bass drum.

French Percussion

Percussions 37 (1994). Percussions Sans Frontieres, 18 rue Theodore-Rousseau, F-77930 Chailly-en-Biere. 37 pages, in French. ISSN: 0992-5082.

This fine looking journal covers matters of interest to contemporary musicians and scholars. Its focus is on literature, pedagogy and repertoire in the field of classical percussion music.

Some members of the Board of Directors for this magazine include J. Delecluse of the Orchestre de Paris,

J. Francois who is a solo performer and musicologist,

S. Gualda of the Orchestre Opera-Paris, Y. Herwan-Chotard who is a percussionist and composer, and J. Tavernier of the Orchestre National de France.

Authors in this particular edition are J. Ferreira (letter about Ravel's "Bolero"), G.B. (The Xylophones of Africa), M. Faligand ("Si Darius and Si Madeleine"), F. Macarez, F. Dupin (Conservatory Percussion), and E. Masselot (Historical Aspects of the Steel Drum).

In addition to letters and articles, the journal contains commentary about new recordings, instruments, books and music scores. Illustrations include maps of Africa, Trinidad and Tobago, photographs of known percussionists and their instruments, drawings for multipercussion organization and instrument design.

Familiar names to the American musician include L. Bernstein, V. Chenoweth, W. England, L. Harrison, F. Hinger, P. Monteux, P. Paray, S. Sadie and T. Siwe. The Percussions of Strasbourg are mentioned often.

Francois Dupin's article on percussion in the conservatory is of interest here. Dupin's family has been in the field of music since the 18th Century, and his work in percussion is widely admired. The article summarizes activity in percussion including various types, such as ethnic percussion, jazz and rock musics, musical theater, orchestral percussion and traditional drumming. Dupin's article mentions technique and styles of performance that are familiar.

There is an impressive bibliography on the xylophone in Africa. Fifty items are listed alphabetically, according to the authors' surnames, and publication dates range from 1929 to 1994. The article mentions also, marimbas, the mbila, general rhythm and tuned drums. The journal's cover artwork depicts a multipercussion setup.

Fortunately, this author has had a composition reviewed in Percussions. The composition is a duo for voice and marimba, titled "A 16th Century Poem." Text is edited from a 16th Century poem from England, and was published so that a male or a female could sing it appropriately. This piece of music was prompted by the Percussive Arts Society, which had run an ad for such a work. Also, professor emeritus and author William Austin had written to this author about my music compositions, and suggested that I write a song. A thorough search for a text resulted in the above.

Finally, the author's surname, Larrick, comes originally from France in past centuries. Legend has it that brothers named, approximately, LaRoque, translating to "the rock," migrated from France to Ireland then to the United States, changing their last name on the boat en route. One settled in the middle west and one settled in the east near Pittsburgh in the United States, and one may have married a Native American princess. The author comes from the Pennsylvania area, born in Zanesville, Ohio, an area rich with people of that name.

German Bibliography

Percussion Katalog 1999/2000. Karlsruhe, Germany: Herbert Brandt, 1999.

This music business deals internationally, and has ordered several of the author's compositions through the years. Following are inclusions in this edition.

4.4.1	- Larrick, Geary. Ballad for Joey, 39.
4.4.2	- Larrick, Geary. Marie: A Four-mallet Rag, 40.
4.4.3	- Larrick, G. Rags' Rag, Scott's Tune, 44.
4.6.2	- Larrick, G. Variations on Just A Closer Walk with Thee, 50.
6.5.4	- Larrick, G. Piece, Piece No. 2, 75.
6.5.10	- Larrick, G. Melody for A. Lincoln, 77.
6.5.17	- Larrick, G. Poem, 80.
6.5.19	- Larrick, G. Waiting & Accompaniment, 80.
10.1.2	- Larrick, G. Quintett for Drumline, 94.

European performances of the author's music have taken place in Germany, Poland and Switzerland. Also, the author's book publishers have offices in Europe. International communication with the art of music is surely a most important part of life in the 20th Century.

Health Ideas

Good health, of course, is important as a consideration for any musician and percussionist. 20th Century miracles of modern medicine, especially in the area of prevention, allow people to live longer and to be more productive with the help of current technology.

Lifestyle for the drummer is important to consider, since the nature of one's work often involves travel to different areas of the world. Thus, diet and exercise are critical components of one's whole repertoire.

An interesting theory regarding health involves percussion music and anger. Supposedly, beating on a drum may relieve a certain amount of frustration in humans. To make the beating an artwork, however, requires highly skilled training and experience. Expression of some kinds of music may lift the spirit, while other kinds of music may not work so well. This is in line of philosophy related by ancient Greek thinkers like Plato and Aristotle. The problem of harmful musical texts toward the young is a present concern, while Classic Period music may in fact effect a more stable mental condition in the listener. The theory behind this is that the music is logically constructed, therefore appealing to the mind's organization.

Further, the logical harmonic and melodic progressions in music of J.S. Bach may have a similar effect. Still, beauty in Romantic music and lightness in Renaissance or Medieval music can have a positive affect on the listener. For the percussion performer, the music is fun to play.

Other concerns of the percussionist are carrying equipment, and being aware of noise levels. Music can indeed promote peace and harmony, and the percussion are capable of producing sounds of beauty.

Finally, the development of ambidexterity is handy for the percussion performer, so that each hand may produce an equal sound. This takes repetitive practice, again an act that can be overdone if one isn't careful. Following is a bibliography related to health in music.

"Aging." Marshfield Ostomy Association Newsletter (April 2000), 1. Marshfield, Wisconsin: St. Joseph's Hospital.

Ard, Ben, editor. Counseling and Psychotherapy, Third Edition. "Theories," Volume I; "Issues," Volume II. Lewiston, New York: The Edwin Mellen Press, 2000.

"Clinical Trials." Mayo Clinic Health Letter 18/6 (June 2000), 4.

Haley, Tern L. "Percussionists' Common Back Injuries." Percussive Notes 38/2 (April 2000), 60.

Heffley, Ph.D., James. "Editorial: Hooray for Our Side!" <u>Journal of Applied Nutrition</u> 50/4 (1998), 99.

"The Internet in Medicine: An Update." <u>Patient Care</u> 33/1 (January 15, 1999), 30.

Kennedy, Edward M. "Changing the Face of American Health." <u>Medicine in A Changing Society</u>, edited by L. Corey, M.D. and S.E. Saltman, M.D. and M.F. Epstein, M.D. Saint Louis: C.V. Mosby (1972), 105.

Mateljan, George. <u>Baking without Fat</u>. New York: Villard Books, 1996.

"Our 2000 Walking Shoe Ratings." <u>Health</u> 14/4 (May 2000), 141.

Perry, Joellen. "News You Can Use: Health." <u>U.S. News and World Report</u> (September 25, 2000), 66.

Shalala, Donna E., Secretary of Health and Human Services. <u>Medicare and You 2001</u>. Baltimore, Maryland: U.S. Department of Health and Human Services, 2000.

Snyderman, M.D., Nancy. "Good Question." Health (October 2000), 166.

Workman, Darin. "Health at PASIC 2000: A New Twist." <u>Percussive Notes</u> 38/5 (October 2000), 65.

Jazz Music

Jazz music is an important facet of American culture in the 20th Century. A colleague of the author, Richard Pinnell, collaborated with me to produce "A Selected Bibliography for Jazz Music" that was published internationally in Seoul, Korea, in the journal Currents in Musical Thought, in Asia. Dr. Pinnell is chair of the music department at the University of Wisconsin in La Crosse. He has performed with the author on several occasions in duo and jazz quartet. The author's experience includes playing keyboard percussion and piano since 1949, often playing in jazz styles. Other experience was playing the drum set in combos and a reading session in a big band, in addition to musical theater in upstate New York.

This extraction from the co-authored work with Pinnell can give the reader an idea of just what is available in print regarding jazz and associated disciplines. Jazz music is a style, often incorporating written melody and harmony with improvisation. Rhythm, of course, is an important part of the whole process. The author has listened to artists like G. Burton in Madison, New York and Colorado in live performances, and has enjoyed professional recordings of many greats through the years. The following list should be a good survey.

Balliett, Whitney. "Profiles: First and Last." The New Yorker (June 19, 1989), 41.

Berendt, Joachim. Translated by B. Bredigkeit, H. Bredigkeit, D. Morgenstern. The Jazz Book. New York: Lawrence Hill, 1975.

Carter, Elliott. "The Time Dimension in Music." Music Journal 23/8 (November 1965), 29.

Charters, Samuel B. and Kunstadt, Leonard. Jazz: A History of the New York Scene. Garden City, New York: Doubleday, 1962.

Cole, Bill. John Coltrane. New York:G. Schirmer, 1976.

Corea, Chick. "Spain." Down Beat XL (October 25, 1973), 40.

Feather, Leonard. Encyclopedia of Jazz. New York: Horizon Press, 1955.

Goldberg, Joe. Jazz Masters of the Fifties. New York: Macmillan, 1965.

Haerle, Dan. Scales for Jazz Improvisation. Lebanon, Indian~i: Studio P/R, 1975.

Hentoff, Nat. Jazz Is. New York: Avon Books, 1978.

Hill, John. "Vibraphone Viewpoint: Red Norvo's 'Blues for WRVR'." Modern Percussionist 11 1/4 (September 1987), 48.

Israels, Chuck. "Bill Evans: A Musical Memoir." Musical Quarterly LXXI/2 (Spring 1985), 109.

Kennington, Donald. The Literature of Jazz. Chicago, Illinois: American Library Association, 1971.

Larrick, Geary. "Gary Burton: 'The Sunset Bell'." Percussionist XIII/2 (Winter 1976), 48.

Leder, Jan. Women in Jazz. Westport, Connecticut: Greenwood Press, 1985.

Lipner, Arthur. "Memoirs of A Jazz Player in an Unusual Band." Percussive Notes 38/5 (October 2000), 61.

Meadows, Eddie S. Jazz Reference and Research Materials:A Bibliography. New York: Garland, 1981.

Russo, William. Jazz Composition and Orchestration. Chicago: University of Chicago Press, 1968. Samuels, Dave. "Achieving Music Literacy." Percussive Notes 38/5 (October 2000), 56.

Samuels, Dave. "Milt Jackson." Modern Percussionist 111/4 (September 1987), 8.

Sargeant, Winthrop. Jazz: A History. New York, New York: McGraw-Hill, 1964.

Schuller, Gunther. Early Jazz: Its Roots and Development. New York: Oxford University Press, 1968.

Stuckey, Sterling. "The Influence of the Black Church in the Development of Jazz." CMS Proceedings 1989 (Missoula, Montana: The College Music Society, 1990), 4.

Ulanov, Barry. A History of Jazz in America. New York: Viking Press, 1957.

Weiss, Lauren Vogel. "Susan Martin Tariq: 'Drumset 101'." Percussive Notes 38/5 (October 2000), 10.

Hopefully this short list of jazz related sources will give the reader an idea of what is going on in the field of jazz. In this time of electronic mail, this author has received some interesting letters from Europe, written by keyboard percussionist Bill Molenhof, a jazz player, specifying musical activity there. For example, Molenhof's jazz group tours widely for performances. Likewise, e-mail letters from Australia, Perth in Western Australia, and recordings, give the author periodically an idea of what jazz vibist Garry Lee is doing. Both of these accomplished mallet players are subjects in the author's 1992 book (Lewiston: Mellen) entitled Biographical Essays on Twentieth-Century Percussionists.

Finally, the author enjoys performing presently on marimba, vibes and piano, often playing jazz styles. Diverse audiences from elementary students to seniors enjoy.

John Cage: Composer and Writer

Avant garde composer and writer John Cage was inducted into the Percussive Arts Society Hall of Fame in 1982, according to a list on page two of the October, 2000, issue of Percussive Notes, volume thirty-eight, number five. Mr. Cage is known as an innovative composer, and one who was very verbal about his purposes.

Some of his music is in regular notation, and some of it is in aleatoric, or chance, style. In aleatoric music, the performer is given notated instructions, with certain boundaries and freedoms. An example of this kind of music is Karlheinz Stockhausen's "Zyklus" for multipercussion solo, where the performer reads graphic notation indicating approximations in volume and rhythm, thus leaving it up to the player to make some of those decisions. This is in line, for example, with a Mozart string quartet, to some extent, where actual notated rhythms are performed not quite perfect, and actual notated pitches are played approximately, in scientific terms. In chance music, however, the range of performer freedom is larger.

John Cage is known as a very successful American composer of the 20th Century. His importance in history is well settled, although not all of his ideas were new.

Bull, Storm. Contemporary Composers. New York: Scarecrow Press (1964), 68.

Bullock, Alan and Woodings, R.B. and Cumming, John, editors. 20th Century Culture. New York: Harper and Row (1983), 117.

"Cage, John." International Who's Who in Music and Musicians' Directory, Twelfth Edition. Cambridge, England:Melrose Press (1990), 115.

Cage, John. Empty Words. Middletown, Connecticut: Wesleyan University Press, 1979.

Cage, John. Music of Changes. New York: C.F. Peters, 1961.

Cage, John. Notations. New York: Something Else Press, 1969.

Cage, John. Silence. Middletown: Wesleyan University Press, 1961.

Cage: "Solo for Sliding Trombone." C. Lindberg: The Solitary Trombone. New York: Qualiton BIS, CD-388 (1988).

Cage: "Third Construction." Pulse: Works of Cage, Cowell, Harrison, Seeger. New York: New World NW-319 (1984).

Cage, John and Harrison, Lou. Double Music, Percussion Quartet. New York: C.F. Peters, 1961.

Cope, David H. New Directions in Music. Dubuque, Iowa: William C. Brown (1981), 56.

Merce Cunningham and John Cage, audio cassette. North Hollywood, California: Center for Cassette Studies-35924.

Gilder, Eric. The Dictionary of Composers and Their Music. Avenel, New Jersey: Wings Books (1993), 78.

Goldstein, Tom. "Recollections and Thoughts." Percussive Notes 34/6 (December 1996), 51.

Grout, Donald Jay. A History of Western Music, Third Edition edited by Claude V. Palisca. New York: W.W. Norton (1980), 750.

Hamm, Charles. "Cage, John." The New Grove Dictionary of Music and Musicians, Volume 3, edited by Stanley Sadie. London: Macmillan (1980), 597.

John Cage, Catalogue. New York: Henmar Press, 1962.

Kostelanetz, Richard. John Cage: Writer. New York: Limelight, 1993.

Kostelanetz, Richard, editor. John Cage. New York: Praeger, 1970.

Music of John Cage and Harry Partch. New York: New World NW-214 (1978).

Salzman, Eric. Twentieth-Century Music: An Introduction. Englewood Cliffs: Prentice-Hall (1967), 164.

I-VI: John Cage, book and audio cassettes. Cambridge, Massachusetts: Harvard University Press, 1990.

John Cage began composing in 1933 at age twenty-one, writing a Clarinet Sonata. Later he wrote "First Construction in Metal" for percussion ensemble. It was this author's pleasure to conduct this work with the University Percussion Ensemble in concert in Michelsen Hall in the Fine Arts Center at the University of Wisconsin Stevens Point, with assistance from Dr. John Baldwin. The author also conducted "Amores," composed by J. Cage, with the prepared piano part done by a faculty colleague who later played clarinet in the Toronto Symphony. A student of the author's directed a performance of J. Cage's "Imaginary Landscape," also.

Thus, the author has had a first hand look at the music of John Cage. I have also studied Cage's solo multipercussion piece, and the solo with a numerical title that makes no sound. The music of John Cage well deserves the recognition that it has received.

Music and Business

The two disciplines of music and business receive considerable attention in today's media. A current "hot topic," is recorded music over the internet, that can be received in a personal computer. As a forty year member of the American Federation of Musicians locals in Cambridge, Ohio, Baltimore, Maryland, Rochester, New York, Central Wisconsin and Madison, Wisconsin, this author wonders if the original perfomers and composers are being appropriately remunerated in this instance. Judging by the news media, this state of affairs is changing and in development. To be sure, there is much good to be done, and much good has been done in the fields of music and business. Following are some sources that are relevant to both.

Apel, Willi. "Music." Harvard Dictionary of Music, Second Edition. Cambridge, Massachusetts: Harvard University Press, 1973.

"Business." Webster's New Universal Unabridged Dictionary, Second Edition. New York: Simon and Schuster (1983), 245.

Catalog, Music and Booklets,- 31st Edition. Stevens Point, Wisconsin: G and L Publishing, February, 2000.

de Souza, Anthony R. A Geography of World Economy. New York: Macmillan Publishing, 1990.

Directory of Music Faculties in College and Universities, U.S. and Canada, 1995-96. Missoula, Montana: CMS Publications, 1995.

"Economics." Oxford Family Encyclopedia, First Edition. London: George Philip Limited (1997), 223.

Einstein, Alfred. A Short History of Music, Third American Edition Revised, Translated from the German. New York: Barnes and Noble (1934), 1996.

Elliott, Raymond. Fundamentals of Music. Englewood Cliffs: Prentice-Hall, 1955.

Larrick, Geary. "Teaching Business Ethics." Small Business Forum 10/2 (Fall 1992), 5.

Larrick, Geary and Kawles, Terrance. "Music as Business: A Bibliography." NACWPI Journal XLVIII/4 (Summer 2000), 7.

"Laws and Legislation." The Music Index 46 (1994), 560.

Steve Weiss Music Fall 1996-97 Catalog. Philadelphia, Pennsylvania: Steve Weiss Music, 1996.

Stodder, Gayle Sato. "2001: A Business Odyssey." Entrepreneur (December 1996), 136.

Music and Sociology

This standard annotated bibliography regards the two fields of music and sociology. The author has participated in conferences at the University of Wisconsin-Stevens Point sponsored by the Center for the Small City, located near the department offices for Sociology and Political Science. In these, the author has read an original paper, performed original music, and listened to others.

Encyclopedias and Dictionaries

Feather, Leonard and Gitler, Ira. The Encyclopedia of Jazz in the Seventies. New York, New York: Horizon Press, 1976.

Hitchcock, H. Wiley and Sadie, Stanley. The New Grove Dictionary of American Music. London, England: Macmillan, 1986.

Books

Adelmann, Marianne. Musical Europe. New York: Paddington Press, 1974. Western music is said to have originated in Europe and moved toward the United States. Thus a consideration of western music history includes Europe.

Birge, Edward Bailey. History of Public School Music in the United States. Washington, District of Columbia:

Music Educators National Conference, 1966. Mr. Birge was a professor of music at Indiana University in 1928. Chapter titles include "The Development of the Singing-School," "1838-1861: The Period of Pioneering," "The Turn of the Century" and "The Twentieth Century." This author was a member of the Music Educators National Conference in the 1960s as a public school music teacher.

Block, Adrienne Fried and Neuls-Bates, Carol. Women in American Music. Westport, Connecticut: Greenwood Press, 1979. The area of Women's Studies is becoming popular in higher education. New publications in 2000 reflect this interest.

Chase, Gilbert. America's Music. Urbana, Illinois: University of Illinois Press, 1987. America, in this case, can refer to the United States of America. The term comes into question when one considers both North and South America continents, leaving the author to work out an explanation regarding details.

Craven, Robert R. Symphony Orchestras of the World. Westport: Greenwood Press, 1987. This is a forward looking title that in 2000 would include orchestras of Hong Kong, Tokyo, Singapore, Malaysia and New York.

Ellinwood, Leonard. The History of American Church Music, Revised Edition. New York: Da Capo Press, 1970. Originally published in 1953, this book is dedicated to Howard Hanson, composer and former director of the Eastman School of Music in Rochester, New York. The author had the pleasure of playing percussion under the direction of Mr. Hanson in an orchestra participating in a new music festival. Ellinwood's book traces American church music history from 1494 A.D., including discussions about instruments, performers, notation and repertory.

Farnsworth, Paul R. The Social Psychology of Music. New York: Holt, Rinehart and Winston, 1958. Mr. Farnsworth was a psychology professor at Stanford University. Chapter titles include "Language Aspects of Music," "Melody," "The Measurement of Musical Abilities" and "The Nature of Musical Abilities." These are certainly relevant today.

Frith, Simon. World Music, Politics and Social Change. Manchester, United Kingdom: Manchester University Press, 1989. This forward looking title combines various disciplines. In 2000, world music and ethnomusicology are popular.

Hamm, Charles. Music in the New World. New York: W.W. Norton, 1983. Mr. Hamm, a professor at Dartmouth College, has written chapters on the musics of Anglo-Americans, Black Americans and Native Americans. Types or styles of music mentioned are avant garde, jazz, popular song and religious music.

Herndon, Marcia and McLeod, Norma. Music as Culture. Norwood, Pennsylvania: Norwood Editions, 1979. Herndon and McLeod taught at the University of California in Berkeley, and at the University of Ottawa. Sample chapter titles are "Cognition and Value Judgments," "Field Techniques" and "The Relationships of Music to Social Institutions."

Hixon, Donald L. Music in Early America. Metuchen, New Jersey: Scarecrow Press, 1970. This is an area worth looking into, as there is not a lot written about it. The Sonneck Society for American Music is interested.

Jackson, Irene V. More than Drumming. Westport: Greenwood Press, 1985. Jackson prepared this book with the cooperation of the Center for Ethnic Music at Howard University. The book contains ten essays on African and Afro-Latin American music and musicians. Obviously, the author's intention reflecting the book's title was that there is a lot going on in that music, more than meets the eye. This is a good argument for the viability of musical analysis.

Kohn, Karl. Music in American Life. Chicago: Rand McNally, 1967. Mr. Kohn, a music professor at Pomona College, has included a bibliography and photos of composers. Topics include music of colonial America, the development of American music in the 18th Century, nationalism, and music since 1900.

Larrick, Geary. Biographical Essays on Twentieth-Century Percussionists. Lewiston, New York: The Edwin Mellen Press, 1992. This 322-page book details the professional careers of eighty contemporary musicians from several countries, emphasizing -the United States. There is extensive bibliography and three appendices. A follow-up book by S. Barnhart, published in 2000 by Greenwood Press in Westport, is entitled Percussionists. The latter book is longer with more subjects, subtitled "A Dictionary." Both books emphasize art and culture.

May, Elizabeth. Musics of Many Cultures. Berkeley, California: University of California Press, 1980. This 431-page book with recording has twenty chapters with essays written by M. Hood and B. Nettl. Subjects include musics of Alaska, China, Ethiopia, India, Iran, Java and South America.

McCue, George. Music in American Society: 1776-1976. New Brunswick, New Jersey: Transaction, 1977. Mr. McCue was a former arts editor for the St. Louis Post-Dispatch. This thoughtful collection has chapters written by Kenneth Billups, Charlotte Frisbie, Roy Magers, William Schuman and others.

McKinney, Howard D. and Anderson, W.R. Music in History. New York: American Book Company, 1940. The fields of history and sociology are generally considered to be social sciences, while music is an art and perhaps one of the humanities. Thus, history and music are a combination of social studies and art, by definition.

Mellers, Wilfrid. Music and Society, Second Edition. London, England: Dennis Dobson, 1950. This volume is subtitled "England and the European Tradition." It contains bibliography, illustrations and an index.

Merriam, Alan P. The Anthropology of Music. Evanston, Illinois: Northwestern University Press, 1964. This book contains fifteen chapters titled, for example, "Method and Technique," "Music as Symbolic Behavior" and "The Process of Composition." The volume's three parts are subtitled "Concepts and Behavior," "Ethnomusicology" and "Problems and Results."

Rachow, Louis and Hartley, Katherine. Guide to the Performing Arts. Metuchen: Scarecrow Press, 1972. The performing arts in general have much to do with music, and specifically, percussion. Drummers are at times not only performers, but also entertainers. Still, the artistic aspect of performance is lasting.

Raynor, Henry. A Social History of Music. New York: Schocken Books, 1972. This text book traces European musical history from the Middle Ages to Beethoven. Its perspective includes solid groundwork in music history.

Routley, Erik. The Church and Music. London: Gerald Duckworth, 1967. In 2000, the church and music are well. Last weekend, this author listened to an oboe accompanied by organ in a Telemann "Siciliana" from the Baroque Era. The music was good for meditation, and interesting in the fact that although it was in a minor key, it sounded happy. I would attribute this to the dance rhythm of the piece.

Silbermann, Alphons. The Sociology of Music, translated by Corbet Stewart. London: Routledge and Kegan Paul, 1963. Discussions include the general, such as "Music and Social Science," and the specific, for example, "The Structure of Socio-Musical Groups." The original German text was completed in 1957.

Slonimsky, Nicolas. Music since 1900, Third Edition. New York: Coleman-Ross, 1949. Part I is a "Tabular View of Stylistic Trends in Music: 1900-1948." Part II is a "Descriptive Chronology: 1900-1948." Part III contains "Letters and Documents." Clearly, a historian looking at 20th Century in the middle of the century, will have a different view from a historian looking at music of the 20th Century from the end of the era. Both views are valid, of course.

Southern, Eileen. The Music of Black-Americans: A History. New York: W.W. Norton, 1971. This author received a complimentary copy of Southern's book while a member of the music faculty at the University of Wisconsin-Stevens Point. Certainly this kind of sharing among publishers and professors is most important today.

Supicic, Ivo. Music in Society: A Guide to the Sociology of Music. Stuyvesant, New York: Pendraqon Press, 1987. This is the fourth volume in the publisher's Sociology of Music series. The book's two parts are titled "The Sociology of Music" and "Music in Society."

Periodicals

Larrick, Geary. "Music as an Adjunct to Education." National Association of College Wind and Percussion Instructors. NACWPI Journal XLI/3 (Spring 1993), 11. The point in this article is that music and education can be considered apart. However, in an educational institution they can blend.

Regev, Motti. "Producing Artistic Value: The Case of Rock and Popular Music." The Sociological Quarterly 35/1 (February 1994), 85. Definition is of course important to sociologists, as it is to music scholars. From both standpoints, artistic value would correspond with cultural importance and humanitarian expression.

"Sociology." The Music Index 45/7 (July 1993), 84. This reference work is found in research libraries. The music scholar and student find it continually interesting. Likewise, the sociology professor and pupil can search for references to follow in the pursuit of higher education.

Sociology of Education 67/2 (April 1994). Just as the field of music can be considered within the general field of education, the social science of sociology can be seen as part of the wider field of education. It is important, however, to consider each of these within their own spheres at times. This contributes to objectivity and knowledge.

The preceding annotated bibliography on music and sociology probably relates historically to the author's first quarter in college, fresh out of high school. The class was held near my dormitory at eight in the morning, and the new freshman soon learned that he had to get to bed at a decent hour in order to stay awake in class. Obviously, the seeds of interest were sown for a lifetime.

Native American Authors

Native North American Literary Companion. Joseph Bruchac, Janet
Witalec and Sharon Malinowski, editors. Detroit, Michigan: Visible Ink Press,
Gale Research, 1998. ISBN 1-57859-046-9, softcover, 486 pages.

This insightful collection of Native American literature from twentieth-
century authors, brings to light many aspects of contemporary life. More than
thirty writers' works appear, with backgrounds in an American Indian heritage
and study in the liberal arts in higher education. The inclusion of Native American
students is of course a current priority at colleges and universities, beginning at an
early age.

A number of tribes are represented, including Apache, Blackfeet, Cayuga,
Cherokee, Chippewa, Dakota, Kiowa, Modoc, Navajo, Ojibway, Osage, Pawnee,
Shawnee, Sioux and Pueblo. There is much sharing of information among the
several groups, with a variety of interests shown.

The book has good author biographies, with birthdates ranging from 1895
to 1966. Both female and male writers are included in this interesting volume that
contains poetry, fiction and nonfiction. The collection is well organized and
understandable. Photographs of the several authors are included, as are lists of
works and publication credits.

An index with titles follows the main text in a volume that offers mixtures
of literal and oral traditions. Organized groups that are represented include the
American Legion, the Gourd Dance Society, the Modern Language Association
and Phi Beta Kappa.

The writers in this collection display good talent. Specific examples of the
numerous characters in these stories are Aunt Ida, Father Buck, Grandma, Harlen,
Momma and Dad. A primary issue that holds the thirty-seven chapters together, is
intellectual consideration of individual and group priorities within a legal
framework. This book is recommended.

News Items

An important part of written history is published news in media like magazines, newsletters and newspapers. Since these media are, by definition, immediate and run on tight schedules, a closer look in scholarly writing is pertinent, enlightening, interesting and insightful.

Following are several items taken from the author's collection of memorabilia through the years. Emphasis is upon public musical performance in percussion.

In the following bibliography, it may appear rather incomplete at times. However, given the nature of the gathering of this information, there is enough extant to warrant further inspection in a book such as this.

The following article titles or lead sentences have been retained, preceding a summary of their content. What hopefully results is an interesting social history placed in the middle west and on the east coast of the United States of America in the 1950s and 1960s. Further, this essay may give the reader an idea of the career path followed by one musician who has stayed within the field.

Autobiographically speaking, the author was born in Zanesville, Ohio, resided in Noble then Guernsey Counties, then attended Ohio State in Columbus. Details follow.

"3 from Area in Concert Band." This three paragraph article noted the 1963 membership of the Ohio State University Concert Band, directed by Dr. D.E. McGinnis. Students R. Eubanks and J. Griesheimer accompanied the author in this item, perhaps published in Cambridge, Ohio.

"Annual Athletic Banquet Held at Sarahsville, March 1." The author played a marimba solo on this date. H.C. Secrest, Noble County superintendent of schools, gave the address. The author's father. C.H. Larrick, was a teacher in the Noble County schools at Belle Valley.

"Band Concert Will Be Repeated This Evening." Directors were R. Eubanks, G. Larrick and H. Max. Music program included "Ballet Pariesienne,"

"Sousa Medley" and "The 1812 Overture." Secondary school bands were the subject.

"Barbershoppers, Others Perform at Caldwell." This two hour program was held in the Caldwell High School gymnasium, sponsored by the Noble County Business and Professional Women's Club. The author played vibraphone.

"'Battle Cry' Entry." <u>Columbus Dispatch</u> (Sunday, October 15, 1961), 3-B. The day following a Saturday football game in Ohio Stadium, this photo shows the Ohio State University Marching Band, including the author as a freshman flugelhorn player, making its traditional entry from the ramp into the Stadium performing "The Buckeye Battle Cry" pregame. As with the other items, the source is from the author's private collection.

"BPW Group Has Dinner Meeting." Reported in Caldwell, Ohio, this meeting took place at Belle Valley High School. The program included G. Larrick performing on vibraphone.

"Cambridge Orchestra To Perform." This newspaper photo and article from the 1960s in southeastern Ohio details a concert conducted by the author. Composers on the program included Palestrina, Tchaikovsky and Wagner. The small orchestra, performing in Central Junior High Auditorium, presented youth concerts at elementary schools, and played for a meeting of the Eastern Ohio Teachers Association.

"Cambridge Student Will Present Graduating Recital at Ohio State." This article is about the author's senior undergraduate recital. It was held in Hughes Hall on campus, with percussion music composed by Kurka and Musser.

"Campus News." <u>Ohio State Lantern</u> (October 13, 1964). The composer of "Across the Field," William Dougherty, contributed royalties from the song in 1954 to a University Endowment Fund, establishing an award. This author received the scholarship in his senior year, while serving as a unit leader in the Stadium Scholarship Dormitory. Performing activities included positions in the Brass Choir percussion section, Buckeye Band, Concert Band, Marching Band, Percussion Ensemble and the Orchestra.

A highlight was playing timpani with calf heads in a presentation of Handel's "Messiah" in St. John Arena. Other memories include playing for championship teams in basketball in the Military Band.

"Canvassing Begins for Directory." One of the author's first jobs involved working for a Chillicothe publisher, L.W. Piercy, manager. This canvassing job lasted about a month in Cambridge, involving house to house interviews with accurate note taking.

"Christmas Concert To Be Given at Local School." This concert was presented in the gym of the new school building on Clairmont Avenue in Cambridge. It included strings, vocal and wind ensembles. A keyboard percussion duet was performed by S. Kuhn and the author on marimba and vibraharp, respectively.

"CHS Music Students Take Part in Festival at Muskingum College." This article noted the Ninth District Ohio Music Education Association Saturday contest that included the author playing violoncello in a string ensemble comprised of M. Amos, M. Burns, L. Dudley, S. Hartman, A. Johnstone and K. McKnight. The group did not compete, but received helpful written comments from the adjudicator.

"CHS Orchestra Concert Set for Tuesday Evening." The Daily Jeffersonian, Cambridge, Ohio (Monday, January 30, 1967), 16. Accompanied by a photo of student violinists C. Heavilin and E. Skultin, director G. Larrick conducted music composed by Bach, Corelli, Gounod, Khachatunian, Schubert and Sibelius.

"Concert Band Plays Sunday at Mershon." This November concert was conducted by Dr. D.E. McGinnis, with the author in the percussion section. Composers represented on the program were Barber, Dello Joio, Elwell, Hindemith, Leyden, Reed, Vaughan Williams, Vivaldi.

"Crowning Moment." Columbus Dispatch (Sunday, October 25, 1964), 42-B. This photo features the Ohio State University Marching Band behind the homecoming court, with the author at cymbals.

"Cumberland-Grange Meeting." The author presented special music for this occasion. An address was given by W. Miller of the county extension office.

"Cumberland Seniors To Present Comedy." This December program in Guernsey County, Ohio, included the author performing music on keyboard percussion, between the acts of a stage play. Directing teacher was E. Hannon.

"Downbeat." Columbus Dispatch (Sunday, September 27, 1964), 44-B. This photo shows the new director of the Ohio State University Marching Band, Dr. C.L. Spohn, a percussionist. The ensemble included the author playing cymbals, and serving as assistant squad leader of L-row. Visiting team was Southern Methodist University.

"First and Second in Talent Show." This two paragraph article from Caldwell, Ohio, reports a talent show held in Cumberland at the high school. The author, then a resident of rural Cumberland, placed third, playing the marimba.

Harriss, R.P. "A Major Symphony's Hard Times and Glory." The News American (Sunday, October 17, 1965), 4-D. This page has a photo of the Lyric Theater, home of the Baltimore Symphony Orchestra when the author was a section percussionist there. The page also lists the week's concerts: a season opening subscription concert conducted by Peter Herman Adler, and a Saturday evening Pops concert conducted by Elyakum Shapira. Music for the prorams included works of Dvorak and Gershwin.

"Here's What the Record Homecoming Crowd of 84,376 in the Ohio Stadium Looked Like." Columbus Dispatch (Sunday, October 21, 1962), 46-B. This photo was taken behind the goal posts at the south end of the stadium during the Ohio State University Marching Band performance of the National Anthem, with the author playing snare drum. The audience sang along.

"How many . . . ?" This item mentions the author playing marimba on the Philco TV Amateur Hour, televised in Wheeling, West Virginia. Reported music was "The Stars and Stripes Forever."

"Issue Message." Columbus Dispatch (Sunday, November 3, 1963), 42.-B. This photo shows the Ohio State University Marching Band directed by Professor J.O. Evans, with the author playing cymbals. These presentations are now on video available from Rare Sportsfilms in Naperville, Illinois.

"Journalism Class Visits Jeffersonian." The Daily Jeffersonian (Thursday, November 30, 1960), 12. Teacher H. McCulley is photographed here with a class of nineteen students, including the author.

"Larrick Gets National Award; Nixon Given Gift." Director D.B. Nixon led this presentation, with the author receiving an Arion Award as a secondary school senior in 1961. Performances were in the county seat of Guernsey County, Cambridge, at the State Theater.

"Marching Along." This advertisement noted a cast of seventy, including the author on keyboard percussion. Sponsored by the local volunteer fire department, it was held in April at the Pleasant City High School building.

"Named To Honor Roll at Ohio State." Winter quarter academic excellence is reported here, including college students W. Gillespie, G. Larrick, D. Noble, J. Rice and C. Rogovin.

"Officers of Garfield PTA Are Elected." This meeting at Garfield School on the south side of Cambridge, Ohio, included a program by the Marimba Music Makers--M. Kuhn, S. Kuhn, G. Larrick.

O'Hara, Mary. "River Rhythm." The Pittsburgh Press (Sunday, June 21, 1964), Section 5, Page 1. This article features activities of the American Wind Symphony Orchestra Women's Association. The author was a section percussionist in the ensemble that summer, along with J. Fedderson, T. Small, J. Gibson and Y. Yamaguchi.

"Quaker City Chapter of OES . . . ." This fifty-fifth anniversary dinner included the author playing xylophone.

"Senecaville - Alumni Banquet." This article in The Journal of Caldwell, Ohio, tells about a high school presentation that included the author performing vibraharp.

Sharp, Fern. "Barbecue Masters Swing into Action at Outdoor Grills.' This nine paragraph article mentions an associated concert of the University Band at Mirror Lake amphitheater on campus at Ohio State, with the author at percussion.

"Sophomore Hi-Y Officers." The Daily Jeffersonian (Monday, November 10, 1958), 8. This photo shows the author as an elected president of the Sophomore Hi-Y organization, with other officers J. Arnett, D. Dickson, D. Lewis and T. Merrill. Teacher H. Hackenburg was the high school group's advisor, meeting at the YMCA.

"Trustee and Clerk's Association to Meet." This meeting was held in the Caldwell Elementary School, including the author playing keyboard percussion music.

"Typewriters in Class Are New and Incentive." This four paragraph article appeared during the author's sophomore year at Cambridge High School, attending in the Central building on Steubenville Avenue. Leading student typists were S. Kuhn, G. Larrick and N. Downs, instructed by L. Anderson.

"'Variety Night' Plans Started." This program was presented in the high school auditorium on Steubenville Avenue in Cambridge, Ohio, including the Geary Larrick Quartet.

In summary, this thirty item collection of printed news from the 1950s and 1960s in Baltimore, Ohio and Pittsburgh, gives one an idea of the scope encompassed by serious musical training. These various events offered the author many opportunities to learn the art of keyboard percussion and music, performed in numerous environments for a variety of audiences. Owning an instrument, of course, is an advantage.

No doubt the author learned something important from the adult leaders of each presentation, as well as becoming familiar with a certain kind of repertoire. Music as art and music as entertainment are sometimes alike and sometimes different. Each program presented a unique set of circumstances and collaborators. Percussion music is diverse enough that it can fit into many programs appropriately. Hopefully this list of news items has shed some light on the art.

News Items II

An important facet of modern music activity is the news reporting about musical events to the public. In professional publications, these reports are crucial for musicians to learn about what others are doing. Also, it is important that musicians get credit for what they have done.

Since the performance of percussion music is a public event, news items in that regard are appropriate, informative and enlightening. For example, composers can get ideas from these reports regarding what is being performed and, perhaps, what is not being done. This can act as a stimulus for preparing new music that fills empty spaces in the repertoire. Thus, reading that music for bass clarinet is rare, may motivate a composer with specific ability to write for that instrument. At the same time, keeping in tune with what is happening in society can give the composer and performer adequate guidance in the preparation of presentations.

Following are several news items from the 1980s to 2000, regarding the author's activity in percussion music and writing. Hopefully these can give the reader some idea of what is happening in the field.

"Alumni - 1970s." Eastman Notes (July 1997), 18. Rochester, New York: University of Rochester, Eastman School of Music.

"Alumni News - Geary Larrick." Music from Colorado (Spring 1997), 12. Boulder, Colorado: University of Colorado, College of Music.

"Alumni Notes - 1970s - Bibliography . . . Eastman Notes 20/21 (Winter 2000), 24.

"Alumni Notes - Geary Larrick." Music at Ohio State 25 (1997-98), 21-22. Columbus, Ohio: The Ohio State University, School of Music.

"Alumni Notes - 1970s - Percussionist Geary Larrick." Eastman Notes (Winter 1998), 35.

"Alumni Review - '70 - Geary Larrick." Rochester Review (Fall 1997), 61. University of Rochester.

"Alumni Review - Class Notes - Eastman - '70." Rochester Review 61/3 (Spring-Summer 1999), 60.

"Books - Geary Larrick." National Drum Association (NDA) Magazine 10/4 (Fall 1999), 12.

"Bravo! Alumni Update - Geary Henderson Larrick." Music from Colorado (Spring 2000), 16.

"Bravo! Alumni Update - Geary H. Larrick." Music from Colorado (Summer 2000), 18.

"Chapter and Membership News - Wisconsin." Percussion News (January 1994), 11.

"Chapter News and Membership News - Wisconsin -Geary Larrick." Percussive Notes 31/2 (December 1992), 112.

"Class Notes - 1960s - Geary H. Larrick." Discovery 3/1 (Winter 1998), 23. - Ohio State University, College of Education.

"Class Notes - 1960s - Geary Henderson Larrick." Discovery 5/1 (Summer 2000), 25.

"Class Notes - 1970s - Terrance Kawles." Pointer Alumnus (Fall 2000), 17. University of Wisconsin, Stevens Point.

"Class Notes - '70 - Geary H. Larrick." Rochester Review (Spring-Summer 1998), 59.

"Congratulations - Geary Larrick." NDA Magazine 4/5-6 (December 1993), 14.

"Congratulations - Geary Larrick." NDA Magazine 8/3 (1997), 14.

"CU People - 80s - Geary Larrick." Coloradan 4/4 (February 2000), 32. University of Colorado, Boulder.

"Entertainment - Marimba Recital." The Daily (Thursday, April 29, 1993). University of Wisconsin, Stevens Point.

"Fellowship Authors and Composers - Larrick." News Notes 37/1 (September-October 1991), 30. The Fellowship of United Methodists in Worship, Music and Other Arts, Nashville, Tennessee.

"Mallet Keyboard Solos with Accompaniment - Larrick." Steve Weiss Music Fall 1997-98 Catalog (1997), 100.

"Mallet - Noten - Marimba Solo - Larrick, Geary." Percussion Katalog 97/98. Karisruhe: H. Brandt (1997), 38.

"Membership News - Wisconsin." Percussion News (January 1998), 8..

"Music - Geary Larrick - 2nd Announcement." New Books - Music, Art, Theater and Film. Bern: Peter Lang AG (Winter 1996-97), 11.

"Musikbucher - Larrick, Geary." Percussion Katalog 97/98. Herbert Brandt (1997), 98.

"People and Places - Wisconsin." Percussion News (July 2000), 12.

"People and Places - Wisconsin-Percussionist Geary Larrick." Percussion News (September 2000), 11.

"Percussion Ensembles - Larrick, Geary." Steve Weiss Music Fall 1997-98 Catalog (1997), 126.

"Percussion und Oboe - Larrick, Geary." Percussion Katalog 97/98. Herbert Brandt (1997), 72.

"Programs of Membership - Wisconsin-University of Wisconsin, Stevens Point, Gesell Institute." Percussive Notes 30/2 (December 1991), 85.

"Programs - Wisconsin-Stevens Point." Percussion News (September 1997), 13.

"Recommended Reading - A Selected Bibliography of Jazz Music." Jazz Letter 9/4 (Fall 1991), 12. Arts Midwest, Minneapolis.

"Solo and Ensemble Recital Programs - Wisconsin -University of Wisconsin, Stevens Point." Percussive Notes 24/5 (July 1986), 54.

Stewart, Trudy. "Percussion in Print." Stevens Point Journal (Thursday, September 30, 1999), C-3. Includes photo of author in basement of new home.

"Sustaining Members - Publishers - G and L Publishing." Percussive Notes 29/4 (April 1991), 93.

"Timpani Methods - Larrick, Geary." Steve Weiss Music Fall 1997-98 Catalog. Philadelphia (1997), 79.

"Unaccompanied Snare Drum Solos - Larrick, Geary." Steve Weiss Music Fall 1997-98 Catalog (1997), 87.

"Wisconsin Chapter News." Percussive Notes 29/4 (April 1991), 87.

"Writers - Geary H. Larrick." 20th Century Music 4/7 (July 1997), 46. Published in California.

George Gard

George Gard

Percussion in Music Education

Following is a short list of diverse sources in the blended fields of education, music and percussion. The reader's interest is appreciated.

Albrecht, Theodore. "Beethoven's Timpanist, Ignaz Manker." Percussive Notes 38/4 (August 2000), 54.

"Book Review - Philosophy of Education." Educational Studies 27/1 (Spring 1996), 62.

Larrick, Geary. "Percussion in Music." NACWPI Journal XLVIII/1 (Fall 1999), 8.

Waites, Bryan. "Introducing Rudiments to Beginners." Vic Firth Education 3/7 (Spring 2000), 1.

Watanabe, Ruth T. Introduction to Music Research. Englewood Cliffs: Prentice-Hall, 1967.

Accompanying notes would say that Dr. Albrecht is a musicologist at Kent State University. Dr. Watanabe was the author's bibliography teacher at the Eastman School of Music of the University of Rochester. Vic Firth is a former timpanist with the Boston Pops and the Boston Symphony Orchestra, now concentrating on education and high quality production. Finally, a strong educational philosophy is imperative for good teaching.

Percussion Repertoire

Following is a series of compositions, identified with their composers, that represent a cross section of music that a percussionist may experience. The accompanying commentary tends to be pedagogical in nature, since the author has been trained as a teacher in addition to research and performance.

Abe, K. "Frogs." This four mallet marimba solo is written by a performer from Japan. It is a piece that has character and wit, in addition to being good for learning four mallet technique.

Albright, W. "Take That." This percussion ensemble features varying sizes of bass drums. It is a good example of what the author would identify as neo-romantic music composed in the second half of the 20th Century.

Alford, K. "Colonel Bogey." This well known march can be effective played by a wind ensemble. The snare drum part sounds especially interesting when played with open rolls.

Anderson, A. "Steppin' 'Round." This solo for xylophone with stage band accompaniment has the form of a novelty rag. It works also on vibes and marimba. Date of composition was probably before 1950.

Anderson, L. "Sandpaper Ballet." This light work for orchestra or band, features the percussion section playing sandpaper blocks. It is good for learning the technique, which is rather unique. The compositional ideas have the contrast of a master.

Arndt, F. "Nola." This well-known popular piece written before 1950, was arranged and published for keyboard percussion with piano accompaniment. Its moving harmonic rhythm is a challenge and fun to learn. A certain kind of musicality may be achieved, since the music is not only light hearted, but sensitive.

Bach, J.S. "Concerto." The first A-minor Concerto of Bach may be played not only on violin, but also on marimba. It is intelligent, enjoyable music that takes work to memorize.

Bartok, B. "Sonata for Two Pianos and Percussion." This monumental challenge includes music for timpani and percussion. Tuning changes are important, and the performer must write in reminder notes in that regard. Listening to the pianos is of course very important.

Basta, J. "Concerto for Marimba." This good piece can be played solo, or with wind ensemble accompaniment. Required technique is traditional and virtuosic.

Bauduc, R. and Haggart, B. "South Rampart Street Parade." This fine Dixieland number is in a rather march style. The drum part is upbeat and fun. Care must be taken with dynamics, so that the drum fills are featured, but the other solos are not covered over. The work has been recorded at a variety of tempos.

Bauernschmidt, R. "Mesozoic Fantasy." In a romantic style of contemporary music, this ensemble piece displays variety in tone color. Its ideas are interesting and new for its time of composition.

Beck, J.H. "Sonata for Timpani." Featuring a concert approach with some jazz ideas, this good work can be enjoyable for performer and audience alike. It is a modern version of a traditional form.

Becker, B. "Lahara." This confluence of Asian and American ideas, can be performed with tuned tom-tom, marimba and violin. The notation is especially interesting.

Beethoven. L. van. "Symphony No. 1." The master composer never really surpassed his work in this first try, in this author's opinion. As he matured, his pieces matured, and remained very high in quality. The timpani part helps with the Common Practice tonality for several woodblocks is enlightening and interesting. The score reflects the title, as does the sound.

Benson, W. "Streams." This percussion ensemble piece is not only interesting, but also fascinating. The visual and aural collaboration in it is effective.

Bergamo, J. "Four Pieces for Timpani." This solo for four drums is an example of the neo-romanticism characterized around the middle of the 20th Century. It is more episodic than developmental, and effective.

Berlioz, H. "Symphonie Fantastique." The timpani parts are fascinating. The work was composed in Europe before 1850 by a master interested in percussion.

110

Berryman, J. "North Iowa Band Festival." This march has a busy and effective drum part. It is good for hand-to-hand technique; accents may be added.

Bilik, J. "Contrasts for Percussion." As a concert percussion ensemble piece, this composition displays variety in tone color. The chime part is especially interesting and effective.

Bizet, G. "Carmen: Suite No. 1." This extraction from the opera is tuneful. The cymbal part is beautiful.

Blacher, B. "Two Poems." This small ensemble chamber music has a sparse percussion part. The vibe part can be played as notated, without improvisation.

Blair, D. "Suite for English Horn and Piano and Percussion." The author performed this chamber work in recital in spring, 1970, in Main Auditorium at the Wisconsin State University in Stevens Point, with the composer in the audience. The unusual combination of instruments is effective and musical.

Boehm, R. "Two Pieces for Percussion." This chamber piece was written by a student of the author's. The literary ideas transfer well to percussion.

Brahms, J. "Symphony No. 1." The timpani part to this 19th Century European orchestral work is effective and beautiful. The author suggests a rather conservative interpretation with moderation.

Breuer, H. "Bit o' Rhythm." This xylophone rag can be played on vibes or marimba, also. The tune is enjoyable, tonal, rhythmic and fascinating.

Brown, E. "November 1952." This mid-century work is improvisatory in nature, in a classical sense. It promotes careful listening and cooperation.

Buggert, R. "Introduction and Fugue." This percussion ensemble piece is interesting and good. It may be accompanied by study of the historical fugue.

Burton, G. "The Sunset Bell." This vibe solo is published in full notation. However, when it is well learned, the performer may wish to improvise.

Cage, J. "First Construction." This percussion ensemble was rather groundbreaking in its beginning. It is well composed, notated and published.

Cahn, W.L. "Raga No. 1." This solo timpani piece is interesting, fascinating and developmental in style. Asian music influenced its composition, in a multicultural approach to percussion.

Caneva, E. "Marimba Capers." This solo piece was written before 1950, probably. Its style is tonal, with a virtuosic approach being helpful. It is popular, rather than classical, music. Quite enjoyable.

Carter, E. "Solo Timpani Pieces." These may have served the composer as exercises in the development of metrical modulation that he later used in his music that did not utilize the percussion. They are quite difficult, interesting and musical.

Chavez, C. "Toccata for Percussion." This early percussion ensemble composition is masterful in its intent and result. There is less infatuation with tone color, in comparison with later works, and more concentration on the basics of good composition.

Chopin, F. "Prelude." This arrangement for vibe is effective and truly Romantic in style. It can be compared well with the preludes of Bach, written at a different time.

Cimarosa, D. "Matrimonio Segreto." This light opera is classical in style. The timpani part is interesting and musical.

Cirone, A. "Study 26." This solo snare drum etude within a collection is good for teaching the orchestral approach to percussion. It is well composed, notated and published.

Cohan, G. "Give My Regards to Broadway." This well known piece in popular style can be enhanced by effective percussion playing. In this case, the drum is usually in the background, supplying needed rhythm.

Coleman, C. and Leigh, C. "Hey, Look Me Over." An effective band piece, this tune can be well played on the piano and keyboard percussion. In hand, the drum section needs to supply a solid six-eight rhythm.

Colgrass, M. "Three Brothers." This percussion ensemble was written in mid-century as a school assignment. It is definitely an experiment that is successful. There is a featured trio of performers backed by the ensemble.

Coltrane, J. "Impressions." This jazz combo piece utilizes improvisation and modal harmonies. The main melody is especially interesting.

Copland, A. "Appalachian Spring." This orchestral work features a challenging timpani part that uses the tuning pedals effectively. The timpani blend well in the ensemble, however, rather than standing out.

Crumb, G. "Dances from Ancient Voices of Children." The concept of this very fine work is a bit sad, yet happy at the same time. It involves one's looking back at childhood, common to most people. The percussion part is in interesting notation and sounds colorful. Professor Crumb's music for percussion is beautiful.

Debussy, C. "Syrinx." This solo for flute works well on marimba. The author had the pleasure of listening to the great flutist Jean Pierre Rampal perform this piece in summer, 1964, at Carnegie Mellon University in Pittsburgh, Pennsylvania.

de Gastyne, S. "Preludes." These pieces for solo vibraphone are modern, interesting and challenging. Other keyboard percussion works by this composer are "Abacus in Trio" with horn and bassoon, and "Quintet."

Dello Joio, N. "Variants on a Mediaeval Tune." The author had the pleasure of meeting the composer in Philadelphia in the 1960s at a Music Educators National Conference. The occasion was the author's participation as a percussionist in The Ohio State University Concert Band for a performance of the composer's work.

Donizetti, G. "Lucia di Lammermoor." This good opera has a full orchestra accompaniment. The author had the good fortune of performing it with the Baltimore Symphony Orchestra in Maryland.

Dougherty, W. "Across the Field." Adopted as the school song of Ohio State University in Columbus, this piece is lively and tuneful. Especially interesting is the snare drum part played by the OSU Marching Band.

Dukas, P. "The Sorcerer's Apprentice." This late Romantic character piece for orchestra has been used with film. Although the orchestra bell part is often asked for at major orchestra auditions, the bass drum part is especially exciting to play.

Dvorak, A. "Humoresque." This well known piece can be played on keyboard percussion such as marimba. It also works well on viola, written in the alto clef.

Edwards, S. "The Drummer's Delight." This drum feature for wind band is fun to play. The solo fills are written out, or can be improvised.

Ellington, D. "Sophisticated Lady." This good piece can be played solo on vibraphone or marimba. It also sounds well with full symphony orchestra, including percussion.

Emmett, D. "Dixie." This well known tune that was written in the 19th Century, is enjoyable. The snare drum part coincides well with the bass drum. The author's preference is to play the bass drum part with muffling of the resonating head, while striking the playing head midway between the center and the rim.

Farberman, H. "Alea." The title refers to the idea of chance, a form of composition in mid-century. Aleatoric music and chance music are the same thing, involving creative decisions made by the performers of this percussion ensemble, in a sense. Thus, what one hears as a result is left open to chance.

Feldman, M. "The King of Denmark." This modern composition for solo percussionist is also aleatoric. Its notation is interesting, utilizing small squares containing graphic figures of varying sizes. The performer's interpretation should be responsible, that is, allowing for the usual compositional elements such as form, development and contrast.

Fillmore, H. "Orange Bowl March." This standard march sounds well with band. The percussion parts are interesting, especially for cymbals.

Firth, V. "Encore in Jazz." This popular piece for percussion ensemble received many performances in the 1960s and 1970s. It is good practice in a swing style for concert percussionists.

Franck, C. "Symphony." This romantic work for orchestra has a delightful timpani part. The harmonies are especially pleasing, with good orchestration.

Frazeur, T. "Uhuru." This interesting music for percussion ensemble is based upon the ballet. The composer's "Rondo for Marimba and Piano" is likewise a delightful piece to perform and teach.

Garland, P. "Apple Blossom." Written for chamber percussion, this avant garde piece gives the listener an idea of timelessness, with only sound taking place. It is an example of the music after mid-century for percussion that emphasized tone color rather than rhythm.

Gauger, T. "Gainsborough." The composer, a percussionist in the Boston Symphony Orchestra, has produced a standard for percussion ensemble. The composition is knowingly written, and interesting.

Gershwin, G. "An American in Paris." This music for symphony orchestra has a good xylophone part. The composer's opera, "Porgy and Bess," has been arranged for symphony orchestra, including a well-known part on the xylophone that is asked at orchestral auditions.

Giron, A. "Party Time." This duo for percussion and trombone, utilizes aleatoric principles, as well as standard notation. It is virtuosic in intent, with a sense of humor.

Goldman, E. "On the Mall." This march for band has a good snare drum part and is entertaining. The composer's "American Ideals" march is likewise good.

Goodman, S. "Scherzo." This light piece for percussion ensemble has a good xylophone part, and can be taken at "lightning" speeds. The composer played timpani in the New York Philharmonic Orchestra.

Gordon, D. "Bali for Percussion Ensemble." This piece of chamber music works; that is, it evokes the sounds of the Balinese gamelan from Indonesia in Asia. The music is colorful, yet notated in standard fashion.

Gould, M. "American Salute." This piece can be played by band or orchestra, and is exciting as well as tuneful. Its rhythm is particularly pleasing, with noticeable percussion parts.

Green, G. "The Whistler." This solo for xylophone is in novelty ragtime style. A number of tempos are appropriate for its performance.

Hall, R. "The New Colonial March." This piece for band has good percussion parts. The snare drum part is especially fun to perform.

Jessel, L. "Parade of the Wooden Soldiers." This light piece was arranged for keyboard percussion. It is delightful to play on marimba or vibraphone.

Jewell, F. "Gentry's Triumphal." This march for band has good percussion parts, of course. Its tempo sounds well just a little faster than a military march, but not as fast as a standard circus march.

Jones, T. "A Child Is Born." This beautiful ballad can be played solo on keyboard percussion. An alternative arrangement would be to add a rhythm section consisting of bass and drum set. Either acoustic or electric bass would sound well. An added piano would make it a quartet.

Joplin, S. "The Entertainer." This piano rag cuts down well for keyboard percussion. One should keep in mind that the original piano part was written for ten fingers, while the keyboard percussionist has only two to four mallets. Still, the melody and harmony can prevail, allowing for some improvisation if desired.

Kabalevsky, D. "Comedians Galop." This has been arranged for percussion ensemble, featuring a fast xylophone part. The music is enjoyable.

Kelly, R. "Toccata for Marimba and Percussion Ensemble." This marimba feature is well written and conceived. The instrumentation is effective.

Key, F.S. "The Star Spangled Banner." This National Anthem of the United States of America, .s especially fun to play on snare drum and cymbals. 'his author's favorite arrangement is that of The United States Army Band.

Khatchaturian, A. "Sabre Dance." This piece or orchestra has a fast xylophone part, involving what percussionists call "double stops" that are 'est played with alternating sticking. The piece has a contrasting middle section that expresses well.

Koninsky, S. "Eli Green's Cake Walk." From the early part of the 20th Century, this delightful piece Las been arranged for xylophone and piano. In this instance, the generic term "xylophone" would have the meaning of including vibe and marimba, as well as the concert xylophone.

Kraft, W. "Momentum." Other good pieces by this percussionist composer include "Suite" and "Theme and Variations." His writing for percussion is exemplary.

Kreisler, F. "Liebesfreud." The great musician left us with music that can be transferred to the marimba with effectiveness. A creative approach to rhythm is recommended, while promoting melody

Kroeger, K. "Toccata for Clarinet and Trombone and Percussion." The percussion part can be played by one or two performers. Source of the title is the Baroque toccata for keyboard, for example music composed by Frescobaldi and Bach.

Lange, L. "September 12." This piece for chamber jazz combo was arranged by the composer for big band, also. The composer is a graduate of the University of Wisconsin-Stevens Point.

LaRocca, D. "Tiger Rag." The author recalls hearing this played by the Caldwell High School Band at summer concerts on the square in Caldwell, Ohio, before the age of six. In that instance, the tuba section had a featured part.

Larrick, G. "Fanfare and Processional." This band piece was written for a composition contest in Columbus, Ohio, in 1967, sponsored by Charles Spohn, director of the Ohio State University Marching Band. The author conducted it in Cambridge, Ohio, at the State Theater, with the high school band in 1968, and later performed cymbals in a performance in Michelsen Hall in the Fine Arts Center at the University of Wisconsin-Stevens Point, conducted by Dr. R. Van Nuys with the university brass choir.

Latimer, J. "Motif for Percussion." This good percussion ensemble piece was written by the percussion professor at the University of Wisconsin-Madison. The music is interesting with good variety.

Lincke, P. "The Glow Worm." This piece was arranged for marimba or vibes, with piano accompaniment. Another name for the glow worm is firefly. The author watched these little insects with pleasure in youth in rural southeastern Ohio. The music is very tuneful.

Lindholm, J. "Toccata for Percussion and Band." This concert piece calls for several percussion instruments. Their performance is not showy, but in the character of a Baroque keyboard toccata, not unlike Chavez's music of that name. The symphonic band accompaniment is tonally modern.

Rossini, G. "Opera Overtures." The Rossini crescendo is studied in music schools, and his music is enjoyed at orchestral concerts. Probably the most famous is the William Tell Overture, although The Thieving Magpie arrives at a close second. Written in the early part of the 19th Century in Europe, the music lives today.

Rzewski, F. "Les Moutons de Panurge." Performed by the Blackearth Percussion Group, this good music is somewhat aleatoric and developmental. It has a story basis, and produces effective aural images in percussion.

Sabien, R. "The Sound of Fish Dreaming." This pictoral piece for orchestra has a good cymbal part. It is a good example of the effectiveness of modern art.

Schickele, P. "Five of A Kind." This orchestral piece has a good timpani part. The composer is known for his humor, as well as his knowledge and talent.

Schinstine, W. "Scherzo without Instruments." This percussion ensemble piece for handclappers, can also be played by a band or orchestra. The composer was a pedagogue and percussionist with prolific production.

Schrammel, J. "Wien bleibt Wien." This German march for band has an excellent percussion part. I would classify it as more classical than popular in style, like a Haydn or Beethoven march, perhaps. The snare drum part is especially effective.

Schubert, F. "Serenade." This melodic piece was arranged for vibraphone effectively. Other well known music of this composer includes Ave Maria, overtures and symphonies. Schubert's Fifth Symphony is a favorite of this author.

117

Shchedrin, R. "Carmen Ballet." This feature for a stage full of percussion with strings accompanying, borrows music from Bizet's opera. The writing is effective, especially for marimba and cymbals and timpani.

Shearing, G. "Lullaby of Birdland." This is one of the all time greats of jazz music. It starts out minor and moves gracefully to major. Highly recommended.

Sibelius, J. "Finlandia." This European composer wrote beautiful symphonies, also. Finlandia is in many church hymn books. The timpani part is exquisite.

Smith, L. "Psalm 95: 0 Sing Unto the Lord." This composition written by Dr. Smith filled the stage of Michelsen Hall in Stevens Point, Wisconsin, in the early 1970s when the Fine Arts Center was being dedicated. The music has a good timpani part.

Sousa, J. "The Liberty Bell." Many Sousa marches for band can also he played by orchestra. The snare drum parts are especially enjoyable and exciting.

Stockhausen, K. "Refrain." Other well-known pieces by this 20th Century German composer are "Zyklus" and "Kreuzspiel." All call for effective percussion.

Strauss, J. "Emperor Waltz." This light orchestral music has good timpani parts, with effective side drum writing. The bass drum part is of utmost importance.

Strauss, R. "Waltzes from Der Rosenkavalier." Richard Strauss produced challenging, at times beautiful music. Its complexity requires careful attention on the part of conductor and performers. The percussion parts weave into a portion of the total fabric.

Stravinsky, I. "L'Histoire du Soldat." This chamber music has a good percussion part. The composer's "Le Sacre du Printemps" for large symphony orchestra, has two timpani parts, in addition to section percussion. Changing meters are typical, with dynamic contrasts.

Surinach, C. "Ritmo Jondo." This chamber music has parts for handclappers, and a good xylophone part. The music is rhythmic and stylistic.

Swallow, S. "Green Mountains." The jazz bassist has also composed "Ajax Men of Science." The music can effectively be played on solo vibraphone.

Sweet, A. "Ringling Brothers Grand Entry." This circus music for band goes at a good clip, as it is said. The drummer must at times hold back, and at other times lead forward. Simplicity is at times a prerequisite, as is developed technique. Essentially, this is music to accompany the circus performers.

Tanner, P. "Sonata for Marimba." This piece with piano accompaniment, also has a band accompaniment. The composer is a percussion professor with composition training. The Sonata is a joy to perform.

Tchaikovsky, P. "Symphony No. 4." This romantic national music has definitive characteristics. The percussion parts, including timpani, are very effective.

In summary, much of this essay is an oral history. That is, the author has utilized his memory, but not written sources other than a list of repertoire and composers. Hopefully the reader will find these comments elucidative, interesting, enlightening and informative.

Modern repertoire for percussion is an exciting collection of a large variety of music from different eras in contrasting styles. Obviously the percussionist is at. an advantage when learning to play different styles appropriately. This is the beauty of percussion now: there is a rich supply of material to show off technique.

Percussion Teacher References

This bibliography is taken from the author's clinic handout titled "Reference Material for Percussion," that was used as a faculty member in the Department of Music at the University of Wisconsin-Stevens Point. In this instance, the list has been somewhat enlarged, with the order changed.

It is understood that one who teaches percussion is thus, by definition, a percussion teacher. Therefore, percussion teachers include band directors, orchestra conductors and studio teachers. References, in this case, refer to publications that this author has found to be good for pedagogy in percussion. The list is limited and rather exclusive, by necessity. Thus, exclusion from this list does not mean that a work is not worthy, but that space doesn't allow inclusion of a comprehensive listing here.

Order in the bibliography is surname of the author, title of the publication and a short name of the publisher. Since this is being duplicated from a previously existing list, other information such as city and date are not included in this instance. Enough information is given, however, to guide the reader toward many good works.

Since the primary instrument of percussion education is the snare drum, references for that instrument shall be offered first. At the elementary level are suggested:

Gardner. Progressive Studies I and II. Fischer.

Lang. The Beginning Snare Drummer. Lang Percussion.

Whaley. Primary Handbook for Snare Drum. Meredith.

At the intermediate level, some teachers use the drum rudiments, and some do not. Thus, there are two listings here. For general intermediate: Gardner. Progressive Studies III. Fischer.

Whaley. Recital Solos for Snare Drum. Meredith.

Whaley. Solos and Duets for Snare Drum. Meredith.

Further, the standard drum rudiments are often used by teachers at the intermediate level to facilitate the development of technique. Examples of drum rudiments are the several rolls, flams, ratamacues, paradiddles, drags and ruffs. Some good examples of literature are: Harr. Book Two for the Snare Drum. Cole.

Pratt. 14 Modern Contest Solos. Belwin.

Wilcoxon. Rudimental Swing Solos. Ludwig Music.

The third level of instruction, called advanced, incorporates further development of technique as well as a look at the orchestral literature. Suggestions are:

Cirone. Portraits in Rhythm. Beiwin.

Gardner. Progressive Studies IV. Fischer.

Goldenberg. Modern School for Snare Drum. Chappell.

Payson. The Snare Drum in the Concert Hall. Payson.

The drum set, or drum kit, also spelled drumset, has been around most of the 20th Century. The development of the foot pedal for the bass drum by W.F. Ludwig and others in the early part of the century, gave way to more freedom and dexterity of the drummer. Thus, the instrument as accompaniment within a combo or ensemble then had more potential for variety and virtuosity. There are probably hundreds of publications for the drum set available, and I am sure that all have their value. Here are three:

Beck. A Practical Approach to the Drum Set. MCA.

Dahlgren. Drum Set-Control. Creative.

Norine. Virtuoso Studies for the Drum Set. Berklee.

The cymbals have been around since antiquity. They are mentioned in the Psalms in the Holy Bible, although there is no written music for the instrument from that era. In the 20th Century, the cymbals graduated from being mere noise makers to an instrument capable of variety in expression. The orchestral instrument, two clashed cymbals, or crash cymbals, is indubitably beautiful, for example, in Tchaikovsky's Fourth Symphony. A more moderate example is the Turkish Music part of Beethoven's Ninth Symphony. In Debussy's Prelude to Afternoon of a Faun, the tuned antique cymbals are an instrument of delicate beauty, much like those in Psalms. It was this author's pleasure to hear the orchestral cymbal playing of artists Charles Owen, Sam Denov, Gordon Peters, John Beck, Ruth Cahn, William Cahn, in good examples of professional percussion technique. A recommended general book for the instrument is: Denov. The Art of Playing Cymbals. Adler.

The timpani, or kettle drums, also spelled kettledrum have been called the King of the Orchestra. The instrument developed from smaller examples used in the cavalry, then transferred to the concert hall. Recommended are:

Firth. The Solo Timpanist. Fischer.

Hinger. Solos for the Virtuoso Tympanist. Jerona.

Hochrainer. Etuden fur Timpani I. Associated.

Whaley. Primary Handbook for Timpani. Meredith.

The vibraphone, or vibraharp, vibe or vibes, is an invention of the 20th Century. The instrument is used primarily in jazz, but also occasionally in classical music. It is a type of xylophone with a keyboard similar to that of the piano, that has an electricity driven tremolo or vibrato and a damper pedal. Its keys, or bars, are made of an aluminum alloy. Two recommended references written by vibists are:

Burton. Four Mallet Studies. Creative.

Friedman. Vibraphone Technique. Berklee.

The educated teacher of percussion may also wish to consult periodicals in the field. Four to be recommended are: The Instrumentalist, Music Educators Journal, NACWPI Journal, Percussive Notes and News. These publications contain articles by experts who do not always agree with each other; thus the reader is given freedom to make his or her decisions with regard to percussion pedagogy, based upon information given in these good magazines from specialists.

Another keyboard instrument that is important for the teacher of percussionists, is the marimba. The marimba is a type of xylophone with wooden keys, although some of the newer instruments have bars made of synthetic material. Ranges and sizes vary, but the keyboard is similar to that of the piano. Suggested are:

Bona. Rhythmical Articulation. Fischer.

Holmgren. Developing Four Mallet Technique. Studio 4.

McMillan. Percussion Keyboard Technic. Pro Art.

Stevens. Method of Movement. Marimba Productions.

Whaley. Primary Handbook for Mallets. Meredith.

The area of multipercussion, or multiple percussion, involves a single player who performs upon more than one instrument. An example of music for multipercussion is Karlheinz Stockhausen's Zyklus, for twenty instruments, one player. A good book on the subject is:

Goldenberg. Studies in Solo Performance. Chappell.

Many colleges and universities and conservatories have percussion classes for those training to become educators. Some percussion class method books are:

Galm. The Percussion Instrument: Some Ideas on Teaching and Performance. University of Colorado.

Jackson. Percussion for Music Educators. Jackson.

Payson and McKenzie. Percussion in the School Music Program. Payson Percussion.

Spohn. The Percussion. Allyn and Bacon.

Orchestral excerpts are important for the artist percussionist. These are percussion parts taken from larger compositions written through the ages. Some examples of good sources for percussion excerpts are:

Abel. 20th Century Orchestra Studies. Schirmer.

Goldenberg. Modern School for Snare Drum. Modern School for Keyboard Instruments. Timpani Excerpts. Chappell.

Hinger. Timpani Excerpts from music of Beethoven, Brahms, Sibelius and Tchaikovsky. Jerona.

The percussion teacher may also consult a variety of reference sources such as:

Beck. Encyclopedia of Percussion. Garland.

Blades. Percussion Instruments and Their History. Faber.

Galm. Discography of Music for Percussion. Colorado.

Peters. The Drummer: Man. Kemper-Peters.

Sources in analysis, biography and technique include:

Barnhart. Percussionists. Greenwood.

Larrick. Analytical Writings. Peter Lang.

Payson. Techniques. Payson Percussion.

The preceding bibliographical listing has included many standard sources that may be of assistance to the teacher of percussion. Again, the list is not comprehensive, but practical. The author has seen and used several of these publications in teaching privately and in class. Another avenue of percussion pedagogy is the percussion ensemble class. These groups often present concerts or recitals in small and large settings. Your interest is appreciated.

Philosophy

Freeman, Robert and Mahoney, Shafer, editors. <u>The Eastman Colloquium</u> <u>on Teaching Music as a Liberal Art</u>. Missoula, Montana: The College Music Society, CMS Report Number 10, 1996.

This very interesting booklet is the result, in print, of a conference held on February 21, 1990, at the Eastman School of Music in Rochester, New York. General editor of this series is Thomas Heck.

The teaching of music as a liberal art is a broad subject that has been under scrutiny for some time. Schools represented in this report include Dickinson College, Eastman School of Music, Middlebury College, Princeton University, University of California at Los Angeles, and the University of Rochester river campus. Authors in this encouraging and informative publication are Samuel Adler, Truman Bullard, Kenneth Levy, George Todd and Robert Winter, with an introduction by Edward T. Cone.

Titles of the respective addresses include "Active Listening: A Perspective," "The Importance of Listening to Live Music," "Multimedia: Connecting the Sound to the Idea" and "Music Composition as Music Appreciation". In addition, there are opening remarks by Robert Freeman, and a general discussion among several authorities in the field of music within higher education. The conference included composers, performers and scholars.

At the base of these discussions is the combination of past, present and future in music pedagogy. Obviously, the college student who is familiar with the music of Frank Zappa will be different from one who prefers the music of Ellington, Gershwin or Josquin. Faculty choices regarding technology and its use in the classroom, likewise, reflect the priorities of each educational institution as well as spending limitations.

An. underlying theme of the conference appears to be establishing a workable definition of music. Indeed, how can the contemporary music professor adequately compare the music of Brahms, Cage and Stravinsky, for example. Further, what kinds of skills are involved with these types of comparisons, specifically in the areas of timbre, form, rhythm, melody and harmony. Third, how does one teach the music of Harry Partch.

This booklet presents many questions and solutions. It also allows unanswered questions, to paraphrase Charles Ives. The book contains impressive evidence of thinking by leaders in the field. Philosophy and the relating of experiences make up an important facet of the publication, as well as suggestions for improvement

Discussions involve, in part, articulation, biographical information, humor, interactive programs, interpretation, motivic manipulation, modulation, narrative, social background and software. Baseball, science and theater are three subjects that are brought into discussion in the context of teaching music with a liberal approach.

Essentially, this fifty-five page volume considers contemporary music teaching from a variety of viewpoints. It encompasses not only music as art, but also music as communication within the context of creativity, history, pedagogy and performance. Fascinating, personable readable and stimulating are four words that accurately describe this fine publication.

This author has taught music appreciation and history in the Department of Music at the University of Wisconsin campus in Stevens Point from 1969 to 1985. The Eastman Colloquium certainly addresses several of the important issues involved in such teaching. In the end, good teacher preparation is critical for substantive results.

Polish Music

The section on Polish music consists of three sections, titled Polish Music, Polish Music II and Polish Music III. I and III are two different reviews on the same book, each somewhat different. This is done in remembrance of a fine Count Basie recording with Ray Brown and Louis Bellson, titled "For the First Time." On that record, the greats play the same piece twice, at slightly different tempos and with different interpretation. A friend of the author once said that we probably never play something the exact same way twice. That is the beauty of music, always changing, yet with traditions.

Smialek, William. Polish Music: A Research and Information Guide. New York: Garland Publishing, 1989.

This hardcover book of text is volume twelve in the publisher's series titled Music. Research and Information Guides. The book contains a foreword, sections on reference and research materials, and a history of Polish art music from the Middle Ages to the 20th Century. Other sections include ethnomusicology, instruments and voice, pedagogy, folk music, jazz, liturgical music, Polish music editions, a discography and an index. The book is essentially a nine hundred item bibliography of two hundred pages, including a thirty page index that has many terms and names. Annotations are included. For example, the section on pedagogy beginning on page one hundred fifty-nine incorporates notes about publications written by Aliferis and Bojus. The latter details a dissertation at the University of Miami in 1972 entitled "Music Education in Poland."

This kind of research and publication is very good and important, especially as we begin a new century. Historians will probably tend to block each century together, for easier understanding. However, some currents of history run through categories, of course. For example, Franz Joseph Haydn was born in the Baroque Era, matured in the Classic Period, and completed his composition career in the new 19th Century. Muzio Clementi is another composer and business person who is .difficult to categorize. Perhaps the sign of historical maturity is learning of minute differences outside of categories, as well as having learned the traditional historical categories.

So it is with Polish music. The popular polka has perhaps a long history, and is a standard today. With intercontinental travel, a Polish musician may go to a new country, taking his or her traditions along.

Polish Music II

In the 1990s, this author wrote a series of articles on Polish music and musicians that were published in GP Light, an English language newspaper sponsored by Gwiazda Polarna with offices in Whiting next to Stevens Point in central Wisconsin, United States of America. Subjects included Chopin, Paderewski, Penderecki and Ptaszynska.

The Edwin Mellen Press, Lewiston, New York, has published a book on Dobrzyski and musical life in 19th Century Poland. The Music Index 50 (1998) lists items on Polish Composers Union, the Polish National Radio Orchestra, and Polish composers. Books in Print 1998-99, volume four, Authors, includes reference to Smialek's work.

Finally, biographical essays on percussionist Marta Ptaszynska appear in this author's 1992 book, and in a 2000 book by S. Barnhart published by Greenwood Press, entitled Percussionists. This author's article in spring, 1995, for the Journal of the National Association of College Wind and Percussion Instructors, also includes professional biographical information on M. Ptaszynska.

The author was pleased to perform Penderecki's Pittsburgh Overture with the Eastman Wind Ensemble, conducted by Dr. Donald Hunsherger, for a published recording. Percussion instructor for the group was John Beck.

Polish Music III

Smialek, William. <u>Polish Music</u>. New York, New York: Garland, 1989. ISBN 0-8240-4614-5, 260 pages. This informative hardcover book is volume twelve in the publisher's series, Music Research and Information Guides. Other subjects are American folk music, art song, the blues, chamber music, dance, Latin American music, opera, performance practice, the piano, popular music and traditional music of Britain and Ireland. The text includes a detailed index and discography.

In the fine publication <u>Polish</u> <u>Music</u>, nearly a thousand items are listed in annotated bibliography. The book's foreword comments on the author's approach to research, beginning with his doctoral dissertation. Primary sections are on reference and research materials, and on history of Polish art music from the Medieval Period to Post-Romanticism or the 20th Century. There are ten references regarding the historic pianist and composer Frederic Chopin.

This author has played Chopin's music on keyboard percussion, arranged and published in the 20th Century by master artists George Hamilton Green and Clair Omar Musser. A related bibliography appears in <u>NACWPI Journal</u>.

Proud Century

Montgomery, Jr., E.E. "Proud Century." <u>On the March</u>, Volume 1. The Ohio State University Marching Band, directed by Dr. Jon R. Woods. Tailgate Records, P.O. Box 600, Wilmette, Illinois 60091 USA (1997), #TCD-108.

Composer and arranger Ed Montgomery was at the School of Music at Ohio State when this author was a student. Remembered specifically was his arrangement of songs from Bernstein's "West Side Story," that had 360 degree spin turns added on the march. Montgomery's arrangement of "Greensleeves" was recorded by the band, with the author playing concert cymbals in Mershon Auditorium in Columbus, directed by Dr. Charles Spohn, for the recording <u>Saturday Afternoon at Columbus</u>, published by Fidelity Sound in 1964, Redwood City, California, LPS-1251. The composer Montgomery is noted for other works that were performed at Ohio State also.

"Proud Century" is written for an ensemble of winds and percussion, numbering over a hundred. The wind instruments comprise various sizes and shapes of brasswinds, including trumpets in B-flat and E-flat, tenor horns, alto horns, trombones, sousaphones, baritones and flugelhorns. Percussion instrumentation encompasses various sizes of drums--some with snares, and several pairs of clashed cymbals.

Montgomery's writing is clear and transparent like that of Aaron Copland, but with different tonalities. Each voice is duplicated numerous times with good intonation and even ensemble. The composer has scored a small number of voice parts within the tonal fabric, resulting in a full, robust sound that can be called beautiful. Treatment of rhythm varies in tempo from metronome markings of about ninety-two to one hundred and sixteen. These temporal shifts are handled well. There are several changes in tempo.

Tempo changes correspond well with harmonic rhythm, melody and sonority. Character of the music fits the title appropriately. Words describing this composition would include bright, colorful, exciting, fascinating, progressive, repetitive and stable.

133

The scoring resembles that of arranger R. Heine at times, while charting its own course at other times. This is a welcome addition to the patriotic repertoire.

Publication Notice

"Analytical and Biographical Writings in Percussion Music." <u>Books in Print 2000-2001</u>, Volume 5, Titles, 415.

"Bibliography, History, Pedagogy and Philosophy in Music and Percussion." <u>Books in Print 2000-2001,</u> Volume 5, Titles, 1064.

"Biographical Essays on Twentieth-Century Percussionists." <u>Books in Print 2000-2001</u>, Volume 5, Titles, 1105.

"Larrick, Geary." <u>Books in Print 2000-2001</u>, Volume 3, Authors, 6169. New Providence, New Jersey: Bowker, 2000.

"Musical References and Song Texts in the Bible." <u>Books in Print 2000-2001</u>, Volume 7, Titles, 7514.

These five references reflect the publication of four books by this author. Notices in this particular reference work began about 1990, spanning ten years, or a decade, from 1990 to 2000.

The author's four books are published by scholarly publishers in New York, indicating a considerable amount of research combined with literary skills. It is indeed rewarding to be able to communicate with readers around the world in this manner.

Publication References

The following bibliographical list of items dates from 1968 to 1999, more than thirty years. The source is <u>The Music Index</u>, a reference work that can be found in research libraries. Examples are the reference area of University Library in the Learning Resources Center at the University of Wisconsin-Stevens Point, and in Mills Music Library at Memorial Library at the University of Wisconsin in Madison.

Presumably this overview of one person's writing about music, especially percussion, will be enlightening, informative and pleasurable to read. The subjects of these several publication references range from analysis to the xylophone, including history, pedagogy, performance and technique.

Likewise, this bibliographic essay can give the reader an idea of the scope covered in serious music during the latter third of the 20th Century in percussion. This era witnessed an increase in scholarship, as indicated by the establishment of a terminal degree in percussion. These degrees may be called Doctor of Musical Arts or Doctor of Education, with majors possible in history, performance, pedagogy, theory and teaching.

Since percussion is present nearly everywhere, there is ample space for study and application of the scientific method to scholarship. This essay should help. Its order is chronological and alphabetical.

"Larrick, Geary H." <u>The Music Index</u> 20 (1968), 831.

"Percussion Instruments - History." Percussion: Its Status from Antiquity to the Modern Era, G.H. Larrick. <u>The Music Index</u> 20 (1968), 1095.

"Larrick, Geary H." <u>The Music Index</u> 24 (1972), 606.

"Marching Bands." Which Marching Band Drumming Style Do You Prefer? G. Larrick. <u>The Music Index</u> 24 (1972), 66'1

"Percussion Instruments - Technique." Which Marching Band Drumming Style Do You Prefer? G. Larrick. <u>The Music Index</u> 24 (1972), 802.

"Cahn, ,William - Works." A Master Lesson on William Cahn's Etude for Tape Recorder and Percussion, G. Larrick. <u>The Music Index</u> 25 (1973), 206.

137

"Larrick, Geary H." The Music Index 25 (1973), 690.

"Carter, Elliott Cook." Eight Pieces for Four Timpani by Elliott Carter - Analysis, G.H. Larrick. The Music Index 26 (1974), 219.

"Larrick, Geary H." The Music Index 26 (1974), 680.

"Dahi, Ingolf - Works." Ingolf Dahi: Duettino Concertante - Analysis, G.H. Larrick. The Music Index. 27 (1975), 248.

"Larrick, Geary H." The Music Index 27 (1975), 541.

"Burton, Gary - Works." Gary Burton: The Sunset Bell - Analysis, G. Larrick. The Music Index 28 (1976), 184.

"Larrick, Geary H." The Music Index 28 (1976), 616.

"Vibes." Gary Burton: The Sunset Bell-Analysis, G. Larrick. The Music Index 28 (1976), 1138.

"Larrick, Geary H." The Music Index 31-32 (1979-1980), 631.

"Percussionists." The Percussionist's Musical Imperative: 1978, G.H. Larrick. The Music Index 31-32 (1979-1980), 836.

"Analysis." Paul Creston: Concertino for Marimba and Orchestra - Opus 21, G.H. Larrick. The Music Index 35-36 (1983-1984), 24.

"Creston, Paul - Works." Concertino for Marimba and Orchestra - Opus 21, G.H. Larrick. The Music Index 35-36 (1983-1984), 257.

"Larrick, Geary H." The Music Index 35-36 (1983-1984), 596.

"Becker, Bob (Robert) - Works." Biography and Analysis of Bob Becker's Lahara, G.H. Larrick. The Music Index 37-38 (1985-1986), 91.

"Beethoven, Ludwig Van - Works - Symphonies." A Study of the Timpani Parts of Beethoven's Symphonies (3), G.H. Larrick. The Music Index 37-38 (1985-1986), 94.

"Larrick, Geary H." The Music Index 37-38 (1985-1986), 718.

"Timpani Music." A Study of the Timpani Parts of Beethoven's Symphonies (3), G.H. Larrick. The Music Index 37-38 (1985-1986), 1261.

"Carter, Elliott Cook - Works." Elliott Carter and His Timpani Pieces, G. Larrick. The Music Index 39-40 (1987-1988), 254.

"Fife and Drum Corps - History." Drumming and Fifing of the Civil War, G. Larrick. The Music Index 39-40 (1987-1988), 490.

"Larrick, Geary H." The Music Index 39-40 (1987-1988), 822.

"Marimba Music." The Marimba as a Transcribing Instrument, G.H. Larrick. The Music Index 39-40 (1987-1988), 905.

"Transcriptions." The Marimba as a Transcribing Instrument, G.H. Larrick. The Music Index 39-40 (1987-1988), 1451.

"Conductor-Musician Relationship." On Musical Ability - Conducting and Analysis, G. Larrick. The Music Index 41 (1989), 202.

"Larrick, Geary H." The Music Index 41 (1989), 520.

"Analysis." Analysis of Percussion Music, G. Larrick. The Music Index 42 (1990), 21.

"Book Reviews - Larrick (2)." The Music Index 42 1990), 115.

"Creston, Paul (Giuseppe Guttoveggio) - Works." Paul Creston and His Marimba Concerto, G. Larrick. The Music Index 42 (1990), 240.

"Larrick, Geary H." The Music Index 42 (1990), 558.

"Percussion Instrument Music." Analysis of Percussion Music, G. Larrick. The Music Index 42 (1990), 743.

"Percussion Instruments - Study and Teaching." .nalytical and Biographical Writings in Percussion Music, Larriçk. The Music Index 42 (1990), 743.

"Timpani - Maintenance and Repair." Mechanics of the Timpani, G. Larrick. The Music Index 42 1990), 987.

"Analysis." Analytical and Biographical Writings in Percussion Music, G. Larrick. The Music Index 43 (1991), 19.

"Becker, Bob (Robert) - Works." Multicultural Music: Bob Becker's Lahara, G. Larrick. The Music Index 43 (1991), 60.

"Bible." Percussion References in the Bible,

G. Larrick. The Music Index 43 (1991), 73.

"Book Reviews - Larrick (2)." The Music Index 43 (1991), 101.

"Larrick, Geary H." The Music Index 43 (1991), 489.

"Percussion Instruments - Study and Teaching." Analytical and Biographical Writings in Percussion Music, G. Larrick. The Music Index 43 (1991), 659.

"Timpani Music." Analytical and Biographical Writings in Percussion Music, G. Larrick. The Music Index 43 (1991), 884.

"Timpani - Technique." Guidelines for the Timpanist, G. Larrick. The Music Index 43 (1991), 884.

"African Music." Music of Africa, Bali, China and the Xylophone, G. Larrick. The Music Index 44 (1992), 9.

"Bali." Music of Africa, Bali, China and the Xylophone, G. Larrick. The Music Index 44 (1992), 55.

"Biography." Biographical Essays on Twentieth-Century Percussionists, G. Larrick. The Music Index 44 (1992), 86.

"Book Reviews - Larrick." The Music Index 44 (1992), 114.

"Chinese Music." Music of Africa, Bali, China and the Xylophone, G. Larrick. The Music Index 44 (1992)

"Larrick, Geary H." The Music Index 44 (1992), 540.

"Larrick, Geary H. - General Works." Composer Profile: Geary Larrick, R.E. Faust. The Music Index 44 (1992), 540.

"Larrick, Geary H. - Works." A Repertory List. The Music Index 44 (1992), 540.

"Percussionists - Discographies." Biographical Essays on Twentieth-Century Percussionists, G. Larrick. The Music Index 44 (1992), 726.

"Xylophone Music." Music of Africa, Bali, China and the Xylophone, G. Larrick. The Music Index 44 (1992), 1055.

"Education." Music as an Adjunct to Education, G. Larrick. The Music Index 45 (1993), 308

"Larrick, Geary H." The Music Index 45 (1993), 581.

"Bibliography." Bibliography on Ethics and Copyright, G. Larrick. The Music Index 46 (1994), 84.

"Book Reviews - Larrick." The Music Index 46 (1994), 115.

"Copyright." Bibliography on Ethics and Copyright, G. Larrick. The Music Index 46 (1994), 230.

"Ethics." Bibliography on Ethics and Copyright, G. Larrick. The Music Index 46 (1994), 317.

"History - 20th Century." Biographical Essays on Twentieth-Century Percussionists, C. Larrick. The Music Index 46 (1994), 449.

"Larrick, Geary H." The Music Index 46 (1994), 556.

"Percussionists." Biographical Essays on Twentieth-Century Percussionists, G. Larrick. The Music Index 46 (1994), 741.

"History - 20th Century." Women Percussionists .of the 20th Century, G. Larrick. The Music Index 47 (1995), 431.

"Larrick, Geary H." The Music Index 47 (1995), 530.

"Percussionists." Women Percussionists of the 20th Century, G. Larrick. The Music Index 47 (1995), 707.

"Women in Music." Women Percussionists of the 20th Century, G. Larrick. The Music Index 47 (1995), 1022.

"History - 20th Century." Canadian and European Percussionists of the 20th Century, G. Larrick. The Music Index 48 (1996), 450.

"Larrick, Geary H." The Music Index 48 (1996), 557.

"Percussionists - Canada." Canadian and European Percussionists of the 20th Century, C. Larrick. The Music Index 48 (1996), 738.

"Percussionists - Europe." Canadian and European Percussionists of the 20th Century, G. Larrick. The Music Index 48 (1996), 738.

"African-American Performers." African-American Percussionists of the 20th Century, G. Larrick. The Music Index 50 (1998), 8.

"History - 20th Century." African-American Percussionists of the 20th Century, G. Larrick. The Music Index 50 (1998), 392.

"Larrick, Geary H." The Music Index 50 (1998), 488.

"Percussionists." African-American Percussionists of the 20th Century, C. Larrick. The Music Index 50 (1998), 646.

"Bibliographies." Bibliography on G.H. Green and C.O. Musser, G. Larrick. The Music Index 51/4 (1999), 28.

"Bibliographies." Bibliography on Percussion with Commentary, C. Larrick. The Music Index 51/3 (1999), 26.

"Larrick, Geary H." The Music Index 51/3 (1999), 171.

"Larrick, Geary H." The Music Index 51/4 (1999), 173.

"Percussion Instrument Music." Bibliography on Percussion with Commentary, G. Larrick. The Music Index 51/3 (1999), 228.

"Percussion Instrument Music - Lists." Bibliography on G.H. Green and C.O. Musser, G. Larrick. The Music Index 51/4 (1999), 233.

"Percussion Instrument Music - Recordings." Bibliography on G.H. Green and C.O. Musser, C. Larrick. The Music Index 51/4 (1999), 233.

This overview of music scholarship from 1968 to 1999, as referenced in The Music Index, reveals quite a few diverse interests within the field of percussion. No doubt the author's writing reflects the thoughts of other professionals in the field, since there is much communication among percussionists. For example, the author has associated with organizations that

141

share ideas and information, such as the Percussive Arts Society, the National Drum Association, the National Association of College Wind and Percussion Instructors, Phi Mu Alpha Einfonia, American Federation of Teachers, Music Educators National Conference, American Federation of Musicians, American Association of Retired Persons, and the Smithsonian Institution, to name a few.

Reviews

This bibliography of review articles concentrates on the author's work as writer. These publications are listed alphabetically, beginning with the surname of the author of the review cited. Following that is the general title of the article. Other information given includes the title of the work reviewed, its publication location, publisher and date of publication. The entry then closes with an identification of the publication in which the review appeared, together with its volume and number indication, date and page.

Range of dates for the indicated publications is 1980 to 1999, two decades of writing about music. It is hoped that the reader will find this bibliographic essay interesting and informative. It is a good example of what has appeared in print professionally during the historical period covered.

Dansel, Georges. "Partitions." Geary Larrick, "A 16th Century Poem," for Voice and Marimba. Stevens Point, Wisconsin: C and L Publishing. <u>Percussions</u> 51 (May 1997), 18.

Ford, Mark. "Miscellaneous Literature." Geary Larrick, "Four Pieces for Clarinet and Sounds," Revised Version. Stevens Point: G and L. <u>Percussive Notes</u> 28/3 (Spring 1990), 84.

Hewitt, Harry. "Contemporary Eastman." Geary Larrick, "Sonata for Bass Drum" and "Trio for Handclappers." Philadelphia, Pennsylvania: <u>Penn Sounds</u>(Spring 1993), 17.

Larrick, Geary. "Dave Brubeck Is Alive and Well in Stevens Point." Department of Music of the University of Wisconsin at Stevens Point: <u>Notes from the Point</u> 8/3 (February 1980), 3.

Larrick, Geary. "Publications." Robert Freeman and Shafer Mahoney, editors, "The Eastman Colloquium on Teaching Music as a Liberal Art," Missoula, Montana: The College Music Society, 1996. <u>20th Century Music</u> 4/8 (August 1997), 46.

Larrick, Geary. "Reviews - Audio." Cielo Y Tierra, "Heaven and Earth," New York: Elektra Entertainment, 1996. MultiCultural Review 6/1 (March 1997), 95.

Larrick, Geary. "Reviews - Audio." "Dancing with the Dead: The Music of Global Death Rites," Roslyn, New York: Ellipsis Arts, 1998. MultiCultural Review 8/3 (September 1999), 100.

Larrick, Geary. "Reviews - Audio." "Deep in the Heart of Tuva:Cowboy Music from the Wild East," New York: Ellipsis Arts, 1996. MultiCultural Review 6/2 (June 1997), 99.

Larrick, Geary. "Reviews - Audio." "Peaceful Planet" and "Rhythm Zone," New York: Island Records, 1997. MultiCultural Review 6/4 (December 1997), 100.

Larrick, Geary. "Reviews - Audio." Reinhard Flatischler and Megadrums, "Layers of Time," New York: Ellipsis Arts, 1996. MultiCultural Review 6/3 (September 1997), 94.

Larrick, Geary. "Reviews - Audio." Richard Horowitz and Sussan Deyhim, "Majoun," New York: Sony Classical, 1997. MultiCultural Review 7/1 (March 1998), 106.

Larrick, Geary. "Reviews - Audio." The Sabri Brothers, "Ya Mustapha," Danbury, Connecticut: Xenophile Records, 1996. MultiCultural Review 6/2 (June 1997), 99.

Larrick, Geary. "Wisconsonian Era." A Celebration of American Music, Stevens Point, Wisconsin: Stevens Point Area Senior High School, Phi Mu Alpha Sinfonia, College of Fine Arts and Communication of the University of Wisconsin-Stevens Point. 20th Century Music 4/7 (July 1997), 23.

Miller-Lachmann, Lyn. "Editor's Shelf - Studies in the History and Interpretation of Music." Geary H. Larrick, Bibliography, History, Pedagogy and Philosophy in Music and Percussion, Lewiston, New York: Edwin Mellen Press, 1999. MultiCultural Review 8/4 (December 1999), 17.

The preceding bibliography of reviews pertaining to work of the author, reveals an interesting variety of contemporary publications. All have to do with music, at least in part, herewith an emphasis on percussion. This unique listing will supply the reader with ammunition about the importance of music in schools, without doubt.

Western music history goes back to antiquity and ancient Greece, traditionally. A new view, however, is to incorporate a one-world view that includes all inhabited parts of the globe, as well as all races and ethnic groups. This area of study, encompassing music and ethnomusicology, offers many facets of enlightenment and information.

Scholarly References

The Repertoire International de Literature Musical (RILM) Abstracts, or International Repertory of Music Literature, is published yearly. The United States Office is in the music library at Cornell University in Ithaca, New York, while the international office is in New York City.

This author has had references in RILM Abstracts since 1987, in a number of diverse areas. As a library patron, I have seen the volumes included as part of collections at Northwestern University in the music library, at the University of Wisconsin in Madison in the music library, and at the University of Wisconsin in Stevens Point at the general library. The publication is available online.

The Abstracts include bibliography, musicology and other systematic disciplines within the field of music. Studies in various languages are reported, including English, French, German and Spanish.

Each entry identifies an author, a title, a publication date, and other relevant information. Several categories are used, such as sound sources, historical musicology, reference and research materials, music and other arts, theory, analysis and composition.

The RILM Abstracts is a prestigious, high quality reference source in regard to music scholarship. Following are some of this author's inclusions, in chronological order.

1987-03748--ap, historical musicology. "Elliott Carter and His Timpani Pieces."

1987-06497-ap, sound sources - percussion. "The Marimba As A Transcribing Instrument."

1988-03517-ap, historical musicology. "Drumming and Fifing of the Civil War."

1989-00698-bm, reference and research materials. Analytical and Biographical Writings in Percussion Music."

1990-09098--ap, theory, analysis and composition. Multicultural Music: Bob Becker's 'Lahara'."

1990-10460-bm, music and other arts. "Musical References and Song Texts in the Bible."

1991-8756--ap, sound sources - percussion. "Percussion References in the Bible."

1992-06143-bm, historical musicology. "Biographical Essays on Twentieth-Century Percussionists."

1992-06620-ap, ethnomusicology - general. "Music of Africa, Bali, China and the Xylophone."

95-00056-ra, reference and research materials. Knowing the Score: Preserving Collections of Music," review.

95-07386-ap, historical musicology. "Women Percussionists of the 20th Century."

97-03066-ap, historical musicology. "African-American Percussionists of the 20th Century."

99-00024-ap, reference and research materials. "Bibliography on G.H. Green and C.0. Musser.

The preceding list includes both articles and books. These articles were published in the National Association of College Wind and Percussion Instructors (NACWPI) Journal and in Percussive Notes. The two book publishers are The Edwin Mellen Press, Lewiston, New York, and Peter Lang Publishing, New York, New York.

Associated activities included performing the Timpani Pieces of Elliott Carter at the University of Colorado and teaching at the University of Wisconsin at Stevens Point. The Civil War paper was presented at a Percussive Arts Society International Convention in Saint Louis, and the multicultural music paper was given at a meeting of The Sonneck Society in Toronto. Several of the biographical subjects are known to the author. For example, percussionist Bob Becker performed with the author at the Eastman School of Music, and with the Rochester Philharmonic Orchestra.

School Program

In 1995, the author prepared a marimba music program for Washington Elementary School in Stevens Point, Wisconsin, with the collaboration of teacher Virginia Liu. During the celebration of the author's fiftieth year of playing the marimba, this related bibliography is offered.

African-American Almanac, The, Sixth Edition. Detroit, Michigan: Gale Research, 1994.

Balliett, Whitney. Night Creature. New York: Oxford University Press, 1981.

Basie, Count. April in Paris. Verve 8012, 1956. Carr, Ian and Fairweather, Digby and Priestley, Brian.

Jazz: The Essential Companion. New York: Prentice Hall Press, 1987.

Coltrane. Impulse 21, 1962. Coltrane, John. "Bessie's Blues." Manuscript.

"Coltrane, John William." The Music Index 46/5 (May 1994).

Great Moments in Jazz. Atlantic 81907-2, 1988.

Impressions. Impulse 42, 1961.

James, Michael. "Coltrane, John." The New Grove Dictionary of Music and Musicians, Volume 4. London: Macmillan, 1980.

"Jazz." The International Cyclopedia of Music and Musicians, Tenth Edition. New York: Dodd, Mead & Company, 1975.

John Coltrane: Coltranology, Volume One. Affinity AFF-14.

John Coltrane: Transition. Impulse AS-9195, 1970.

Jones, Thad. "A Child Is Born." Manuscript.

Kenney, William. Chicago Jazz. New York: Oxford University Press, 1993.

Larrick, Geary and Pinnell, Richard. "A Selected Bibliography for Jazz Music." Currents in Musical Thought II (1993), 529.

McRae, Barry. The Jazz Handbook. Boston: G.K. Hall, 1989.

Miles Davis at Carnegie Hall. Columbia CS-8612, 1961.

Nanry, Charles. American Music: From Storyville to Woodstock. New Brunswick: Transaction, 1972.

Reference Library of Black America, Book III. New York: Bellwether Publishing, 1971.

'Round about Midnight. Columbia CL-949, 1956.

Sahara. Milestone 9039, 1972.

Schuller, Gunther. Early Jazz. New York: Oxford University Press, 1968.

Slonimsky, Nicolas. Baker's Biographical Dictionary of Musicians, Eighth Edition. New York: Schirmer Books, 1992.

Stambler, Irwin. Encyclopedia of Popular Music. New York: St. Martin's Press, 1965.

Stearns, Marshall. The Story of Jazz. New York: Oxford University Press, 1967.

Stuckey, Sterling. "The Influence of the Black Church in the Development of Jazz." The College Music Society (CMS) Proceedings, 1989 (1990), 4.

Thad Jones--Mel Lewis Live at the Village Vanguard. Solid State 18016, 1967.

Tyner, McCoy. "Three Flowers." Manuscript.

Vian, Boris. Chronigues de Jazz. France: La Jeune Parque, 1967.

This bibliography includes books, articles and recordings. Your interest is appreciated.

Siwe's Book

Siwe, Thomas, editor. <u>Percussion Ensemble and Solo Literature</u>. Champaign, Illinois: Media Press, 1993.

Professor Thomas Siwe taught percussion at the University of Illinois. It was this author's pleasure to meet him in Chicago at the Midwest Band and Orchestra Clinic, when the Percussive Arts Society conferred. The Solo volume contains several of the author's works, listed by composer, title, date, instrument, accompaniment, and publisher, beginning on page 353.

This very important publication lists the author's compositions as follows: "Adagio with Accompaniment," "Aeolian," "Ballad for JB," "Ballad for Joey" (1987), "Ballad for Joey" (1989), "Boston in February," "Composition for Snare Drum," "Composition No. 2," "Composition No. 3," "Dance in Time," "Duo Sonata," "Ecclesiasticus," "Elegie," "Elegy and Meditation," "Episode," "Marie," "Melody for Abraham Lincoln," "A Musical Joke," "Piece for Flute and Drums," "Piece No. 2,' "Rags' Rag," "Scott's Tune," "Sonata for Bass Drum," "Sonata No. 7," "Twojazz," "Variations on Handel's 'Halifax'," and "Vivo Duo." Other composers mentioned include Larsen, Larson, Larsson and Laske.

Sociology and Music

Sociology can be defined as the study of social groups. Music can be defined as an aural art. Further, percussion can be defined as music sounded by instruments that are hit or struck.

Therefore, several related areas of instruction and study come into view. For example, the study of the samba in Brazil can be perceived with sociological overtones, while the actual music may be primarily percussive in nature. Thus the relatively new field of ethnomusicology would have elements of not only music, but also social science. Since there are percussion instruments played in nearly all cultures, a consideration of the literature related to sociology and music would include percussion.

The following thirty item bibliography illuminates these ideas, with a view toward multiculturalism in music and percussion. Percussion is played in the orchestras of Europe, Japan and Malaysia, and appears in the elementary school classroom in the United States. Indeed, Native Americans consider the drum as important in ceremony and social occasions. For example, the Lawrence University Percussion Ensemble in eastern Wisconsin performs on marimbas, brake drums, timpani or kettle drums, bass drum, snare drum and orchestra bells.

Craven, Robert R. Symphony Orchestras of the World. Westport: Greenwood Press, 1987.

Ellinwood, Leonard. The History of American Church Music. New York: Da Capo Press, 1970.

Farnsworth, Paul R. The Social Psychology of Music. New York: Holt, Rinehart and Winston, 1958.

Frith, Simon. World Music, Politics and Social Change. Manchester, United Kingdom: Manchester University Press, 1989.

Hamm, Charles. Music in the New World. New York: W.W. Norton, 1983.

Jackson, Irene V. More than Drumming. Westport, Connecticut: Greenwood Press, 1985.

Kahn, Karl . Music in American Life. Chicago, Illinois: Rand   McNally, 1967.

Larrick, Geary. Biographical Essays on Twentieth-Century Percussionists. Lewiston, New York: The Edwin Mellen Press, 1992.

Larrick, Geary. "Musical Activity in the Small City and Regional Community." The Small City and Regional Community, Volume 11, edited by Robert Wolensky and Edward Miller. Stevens Point, Wisconsin: Foundation Press (1995), 249.

McKinney, Howard D. and Anderson, W.R. Music in History. New York, New York: American Book Company, 1940.

Mellers, Wilfrid. Music and Society. London, England: Dennis Dobson, 1950.

Merriam, Alan P. The Anthropology of Music. Evanston, Illinois: Northwestern University Press, 1964.

Rachow, Louis and Hartley, Katherine. Guide to the Performing Arts. Metuchen:Scarecrow Press, 1972.

Raynor, Henry. A Social History of Music. New York: Schocken Books, 1972.

Regev, Motti. "Producing Artistic Value: The Case of Rock and Popular Music." The Sociological Quarterly 35/1 (February 1994), 85.

Routley, Erik. The Church and Music. London: Gerald Duckworth, 1967.

Silbermann, Aiphons. Translated by Corbet Stewart. The Sociology of Music. London: Routledge and Kegan Paul, 1963.

Slonimsky, Nicolas. Music since 1900. New York: Coleman-Ross, 1949.

"Sociology." The Music Index 45/7 (July 1993), 84.

Sociology of Education 67/2 (April 1994).

Southern, Eileen. The Music of Black Americans: A History. New York: W.W. Norton, 1971.

Supicic, Ivo. Music in Society: A Guide to the Sociology of Music. Stuyvesant, New York: Pendragon Press, 1987.

Thompson, Ryan. The Fiddler's Almanac. Newmarket, New Hampshire: Captain Fiddle Publications, 1985.

In conclusion, a scan of the literature in the field related to sociology and music reveals an interesting variety of selection. Percussion is a part of it all.

Tabla Virtuoso

Sahai, Pandit Sharda. Tabla Virtuoso. Notes by Bob Becker. Published and distributed by Xylomusic, Toronto, Ontario, Canada. World Records WRC1-3045, 1983.

This enjoyable recording is dedicated to the artist's great-great-grandfather, Pandit Ram Sahai (1780-1826), who was also a tabla drum player and composer. The beautiful sounding drums on this recording are accompanied by a harmonium that sounds the melody. The two drums are carefully tuned, and played with the hands and fingers. One could comparatively say that the tabla drums are the piano of the drum world, having a repertoire that is historic, traditional, and impressively rhythmic.

In this fine presentation, dynamics, tempo and rhythmic density vary in musical fashion. Composition types include the mohara, rela, tukras and uthan. Approaches to musical form include development of idea, improvisation, and theme with variations. The artist's technique on the tabla drums flows with good tone. The harmonium player is Bob Becker, founding member of Nexus ensemble.

Tambourine Technique

Larrick, Geary H. "On the Technical Side." Music by James L. Moore, photos by John Anderson. <u>Percussive Notes</u> 8/3 (Spring 1970), 21.

This article was developed with the aid of Eastman School of Music percussion professor John H. Beck, timpanist in the Rochester Philharmonic Orchestra. One of the author's duties as a graduate assistant at the Eastman School, was to instruct the percussion education methods classes occasionally, on the graduate and undergraduate levels. The technique developed was delineated in the above article.

In 1997 when the author was preparing for an audition in Pittsburgh for the Malaysian Philharmonic Orchestra, I read this article as a refresher. It is available on microfilm in the periodicals area of University Library in the Learning Resources Center at the University of Wisconsin-Stevens Point. Thus, when the author was asked to sightread on tambourine at the Byham Theater on stage in Pennsylvania, the review was valuable. The photos were taken in the percussion studio on the third floor of Old Main at the university in Stevens Point.

The Timpani

Kettle drums have a long history in western music. Following are some contemporary sources for this study.

Adato, Joseph and Judy, George, editors. "Timpany." The Percussionist's Dictionary. Melville, New York: Beiwin-Mills (1984), 35.

Albrecht, Theodore. "Beethoven's Timpanist, Ignaz Manker." <u>Percussive Notes</u> 38/4 (August 2000), 54.

Blades, James. "Kettledrums." <u>Percussion Instruments and Their History</u>. London: Faber and Faber (1984), 226.

Bowles, Edmund A. "The Kettledrum." <u>Encyclopedia of Percussion</u>, edited by J.H. Beck. New York: Garland (1995)

Even the tabla drums include a small kettle drum. During the summer of 2000, the author composed "Lamentation for Drum." This piece can be performed traditionally on a snare drum muffled, that is, with the snares off, or with a hand drum, or with a single kettledrum.

Vibraphone Review

Ted Piltzecker: Destinations. Ted Piltzecker, vibraphone, composer and arranger. Jack Wilkins, guitar. Andy Simkins, bass. Ted Moore, percussion. Bryn Mawr, California: Sea Breeze Record Company and Corner Mushroom Music, SB-2027, 1985.

Additional musicians on this melodious and rhythmic recording are David Dando, Jan Garrett, Richard Hathaway, Bill Jackson and Brian Savage. Ted Piltzecker has presented clinics in addition to performing, and has coordinated the jazz program at the Aspen Music Festival.

This recording also includes flute, saxophone, synthesizer, trumpet and voice. It originated in Aspen, Colorado.

The author had the pleasure of hearing Piltzecker perform in Aspen one summer. His four-mallet playing on the vibe is rhythmic, lively and colorful. This recording contains the compositions 'Ashcroft," "Columbus Avenue Strut," "Homesick," "Toys" and others. The recording displays a true sound of the vibraphone, with good dynamic balance among the various instruments.

This is a good example of what the instrument can do in the hands of an entrepreneur. Highly recommended.

Whitaker's

"Larrick, Geary." <u>Whitaker's Books in Print 2000</u>. London, England,
2000.

This reference work from the United Kingdom has many entries, including
three for this author. The three books that are listed are entitled Bibliography,
History, Pedagogy and Philosophy in Music and Percussion; Biographical Essays
on Twentieth-century Percussionists: Musical References and Song Texts in the
Bible. The books were published in 1999, 1992 and 1990, respectively.

Some time ago this author asked a music librarian to find library holdings
for the author's publications in a regional area, the Midwest. It was surprising and
rewarding to find many locations and collections that had the author's writing in
publication. This is perhaps an extension of teaching, since that is what the author
was originally trained for and practiced.

Original scholarship including writing is an important part of today's
society. In publication, it can reach an audience that includes not only the school
system, but also those who are outside schools. The addition of international
distribution makes a situation where one person can communicate with many
individuals in near and distant locations.

Who's Who

"Larrick, Geary Henderson." Who's Who in the Midwest 1996-1997, 371.

"Larrick, Geary Henderson." Who's Who in Entertainment 1998-1999, 421.

These accurate biographical sketches share space with many individuals who are distinguished and successful in their endeavours. These include a state supreme court justice, an actress, a museum director and a publisher.

There are several Who's Who reference books, and they all serve an important record of activity in society. The many articles are interesting from the standpoint that an individual person may have aspects in common with other people included and who may read the article. It is thus a supporting environment for one to read that he or she has much in common with others known or unknown.

Finally, the references serve as a history of society and its specific content. These books are recommended.

Women's History

March is Women's History Month. The area of women's studies is recognized at the university level of education. This author first was introduced to the area of study when it was mentioned by a faculty colleague in the Department of Music at the University of Wisconsin-Stevens Point in the early 1980s.

In 1990, the author was doing research for a book that was published in 1992 by The Edwin Mellen Press in Lewiston, New York. Title of the book is Biographical Essays on Twentieth-Century Percussionists. The volume contains information about the professional endeavors of eighty musicians, including several women.

The spring, 1995, issue of the National Association of College Wind and Percussion Instructors (NACWPI) Journal, associated with the Music Educators National Conference, contained an article by this author titled "Women Percussionists of the 20th Century." Subjects in the article are K. Abe, R. Cahn, V. Chenoweth, P. Cuip, P. Dash, V. Jenks, K.E. Pershing and M. Ptaszynska. These eight percussionists are leaders in their field.

A reference for that article appears in the 1995 Repertoire International de Litterature Musicale (RILM) Abstracts, number 95-07386-ap, in the field of historical musicology. The United States office for RILM is in Ithaca, New York, at Cornell University.

Other references for that article appear in The Music Index 47 (1995). In this reference work, each of the eight women subjects is referenced alphabetically under her surname. Citations are also included on the topics "History - 20th Century, Women Percussionists," "Percussionists" and "Women in Music, Women Percussionists."

In 1999, another book by this author was published in New York with The Edwin Mellen Press, entitled Bibliography, History, Pedagogy and Philosophy in Music and Percussion (ISBN 0-7734-8165-6). This volume is number sixty-two in the publisher's series headed "Studies in the History and Interpretation of Music." A review for this book appeared in the December, 1999, issue of

MultiCultural Review, in the Editor's column, indicating the inclusion of material about women percussionists.

This book, referenced in Books in Print 1999-2000, contains several bibliographical items authored, co-authored or edited by women in the book's first section subtitled "Bibliographic Essays in Percussion."

In the book's third section, "Scholarship in Music," an essay titled "20th Century Women Percussionists," incorporates material about the eight musicians mentioned previously. This discussion includes the subjects' teachers, associated schools and musical organizations, as well as other information of professional interest.

The essay in the 1999 book was read at an open reading by this author on January 27, 2000, for the literary arts series titled The Clear Sun in Scrubbed Sky, in Stevens Point at the Mission Coffee House. The series is directed by English professor William Lawlor. Further, a news item regarding that offering appears in the May, 2000, edition of Percussion News in the "People and Places" column, edited by Teresa Peterson. This item is under the heading "Wisconsin."

In conclusion, the decade encompassing the years 1990 to 2000 have been productive for this author, in regard to research and writing in the area of women's history. The field of percussion music is open with communication among its practitioners. For example, the author has attended Percussive Arts Society conferences for decades, writing for and reading Percussionist and Percussive Notes many times since 1966.

Conclusion

This percussionist's guide to music in the form of bibliographic essays, details specific scholarship in the 20th Century. At one time, the Percussive Arts Society termed the era as the Golden Age of Percussion. This is in part true.

As related by the sources listed in this volume, there has indeed been a remarkable growth of percussion through the past several decades. The growth, as with any progression, has had its ups and downs, its peaks and valleys, so to speak. However, according to an accepted educational theory, the downs or valleys may perhaps actually be an apparent stagnation that is necessary for further growth.

This happens with individuals as well as with societal movements. There are time periods when it appears that nothing is happening. Then all of a sudden, there will be a full flowering of success. This success is based, however, upon the simmering of knowledge in a dormant form.

An example in my own life involves my daughter's learning to swim. She took lessons from experts early in life, but couldn't swim. However, when she was ready, with me in the YMCA pool watching her every move, she all of a sudden learned to swim.

So it is with percussion history. During the 20th Century, there were highs and lows in regard to apparent progression of activity. I would propose, however, that during the lows, there was important change taking place, and that the highs merely reflected that progression.

Examples of high points include Stravinsky's compositions, "Le Sacre du Printemps" and "L'Histoire du Soldat," Varese's "Ionisation," Cage's discoveries, and the emergence of percussion scholarship as shown by the establishment of the doctorate in percussion, as well as the appearance of the solo percussion sonata. These historic events were the results of years of preparation, and represent work on the part of many people, not just the specified authors. In a sense, it was like a political process, where a figure head speaks for the populace through his or her interpreters.

Thus, at the beginning of a new millennium, the field of percussion is noticed worldwide and respected for its diversity, its consistent rhythm and tone color. Hopefully this book has shown the reader where much of the movement's progression took place, intellectually. The history of ideas is unique to human beings, while spiritually backed by a greater power. Indeed, the miracle of life fortunately offers us the percussion.

Bibliography

Apel, Willi. Harvard Dictionary of Music. Cambridge, Massachusetts: Harvard University Press, 1968.

Hampton, Lionel. Hamp. New York: Warner Books, 1989. An autobiography with James Haskins.

Kamien, Roger, editor. The-Norton Scores: An Anthology for Listening. Volume II: Schubert to Glass. New York: W.W. Norton, 1984.

La Rue, Jan. Guidelines for Style Analysis. New York: W.W. Norton, 1970.

McKay, George Frederick. Creative Orchestration. Boston: Allyn and Bacon, 1963.

Partch, Harry. Genesis of a Music. New York: Da Capo Press, 1979.

Plan for Health, Spring, 2001. Marshfield, Wisconsin: Security Health Plan.

Randel, Don Michael. Harvard Concise Dictionary of Music. Cambridge, Massachusetts: Belknap press, 1998.

Sousa, John Philip. The Trumpet and Drum. Cleveland, Ohio: Ludwig Music, 1985.

Straus, Joseph N. "The 'Anxiety of Influence' in Twentieth-Century Music." The Journal of Musicology IX/4 (Fall 1991), 430.

Weiner, Richard. "The Campanelli Part to Prokofiev's Piano Concerto No. 1." Percussive Notes 39/2 (April 2001), 50.

Wesley, John and Wesley, Charles. Songs and Sermons. London: Fount, 1996.

Index

Paris 24,75
Partch, H. 36
Penderecki, K. 129
piccolo 57
Piston, W. 46
Pittsburgh 21,97
poem 76,93
pointillism 59
polka 128
Portage County 14,52
Princeton University 125
Pustjens, J. 33
ragtime 56
Randel, D.,39
Richeson, D. 43
Rochester Philharmonic 15,45
rondo 54
Sachs, K. 35
Scoville, J. 35
Seremban 51
Sibelius, J. 97,118
South America 65,89
Stockhausen, K. 65
Stravinsky, I. 118
Tabla 15
Tchaikovsky, P. 68,96
Toronto 68
University Of Miami 53
Varese, E.65
Vivaldi, A. 97
Vore, V. 47
Wagner, R. 67
wind chimes 55
world music 7,88
xylophone 15,52
YMCA 99
youth concert 41